SECRET MENTAL POWERS:

MIRACLE OF MIND MAGIC

FRANK RUDOLPH YOUNG

parkerpub.co

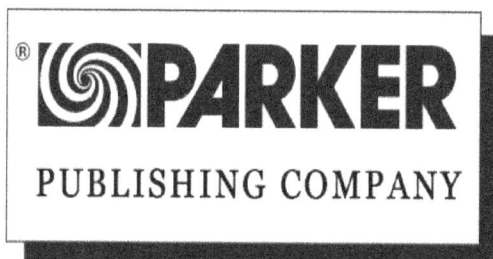

PARKER

PUBLISHING COMPANY

parkerpub.co

© Copyright 1973 by Frank Rudolph Young

Published by Parker Publishing Company

www.parkerpub.co

What This Book Can Do for You

Frank Young discovered that some persons had cured themselves of seemingly incurable diseases, simply with a secret mental power. When he was in business he had already discovered that some persons had become multimillionaires with a secret mental power. When he was a competing athlete he had discovered that some of them had broken world records with a secret mental power. When he was on the stage he had discovered that some actors and actresses had become stage idols with a secret mental power. As an author he had discovered that some writers had conceived best-sellers with a secret mental power. As a research student in several leading colleges and universities he had discovered that some students easily won big scholarships with a secret mental power. As an investor he had discovered that some ordinary people without formal training picked out fast-growth stocks with a secret mental power. In practically everything in life, in fact, there were people who reaped astronomical successes with a secret mental power, with which they easily swept past seemingly insurmountable obstacles. Frank Young decided to find the miracle trigger of their successful mind magic.

The Search for the Miracle Trigger

For twenty-five years Frank Young studied and refined the different methods which so many of these people used to achieve their ends. But, he found, it was not only the methods they used that counted, but *how* they "triggered" them. Without the right trigger they could not even start to get benefits. With his special scientific knowledge of the mind and body, Young experimented for years until he unravelled the secret of the unsuspected power of the *conscious mind*—a power which hundreds of leading scientific investigators have discovered is equal to, and *even greater than*, that of hypnosis, psychic power, the computer, brain-wave machines, or whatever. But it needed the right trigger! That's when Frank Young discovered the secret *Miracle Mind Magic Stimulator.* He confided it to hundreds of people and was amazed at the successful results these people secured for themselves.

The Secret of the Miracle Mind Magic Stimulator

With the *Miracle Mind Magic Stimulator*, otherwise average people achieved "miracles" in attaining wealth, in their careers, in social life, in marriage, in controlling their nervous tensions and worries, in profitable concentration of mind, in controlling others, in self-protection, in wise future action, in popularity, in sensible judgment, in timing perfectly in life, in routing nagging pains and minor illnesses, in regaining sexual vitality, in mastering new skills, and in self-rejuvenation. With it they achieved "miracles" which others rivalled only with brain-splitting effort, incredible luck, or fantastic psychic power. Yet, with the Miracle Mind Magic Stimulator, these otherwise average people achieved incredible successes with their secret mental powers.

In order for them to use the Miracle Mind Magic Stimulator in a natural manner, Young taught them how to flood themselves with their fondest dreams in an instant, so that their bodies would respond to them in physiological language. These people then simply drew this tissue language into their *conscious* minds, and their powers for immediate success *in anything whatsoever* multiplied fantastically.

With secret mental powers *you don't have to tap your subconsicous mind, resort to hypnosis, or strain to develop tension-creating will power.* Once you trigger your conscious mind with the Miracle Mind Magic Stimulator as set out in this book, your nerves, your glands, your muscles, your actions, will be given the *big, invisible push* to hurl you into *successful action.*

What People Like You Have Achieved with the Miracle Mind Magic Stimulator

With Dr. Young's secret Miracle Mind Magic Stimulator,

people like you have started accomplishing *all that seemed impossible for them before.* Here are some typical examples:

1. How businessman Donald Z. came back from disaster to make far more money — and easier than ever.
2. How Steve K. made seemingly miraculous repairs and grew rich.
3. How John B. tamed his giant accoster in the flick of an eye.
4. How laid-off Leo D. constructed a practical article for teen-age play and retired permanently from his job.
5. How hesitant Jack M. turned into a rousing speaker in an instant.
6. How Stanley V. subdued his ulcers with a routing thought.
7. How Marcia L. controlled her "nerves" by lowering her heart rate with a compelling picture-thought.
8. How trampled-down Harry B. aroused the keen respect of his overbearing superiors—and was soon promoted into an executive position.
9. How Donna M. freed herself from a devilish love enslavement, and married a man who adored her.
10. How homely, middle-aged, ignored Sarah P. made an attractive $70,000-a-year income man see her as a ravishing young beauty.
11. How Esther F. ended the suicidal tendency of her failing college student son and raised him to the honor roll.
12. How Bill K. saved himself from a long, disastrous layoff by enthralling his greatest enemy swiftly.
13. How Elmer T., on the verge of legal catastrophe, recalled neglected vital evidence suddenly and saved himself.
14. How Larry N. raised his I.Q. into that of an executive genius in seconds.
15. How Austin J. led his company into amazing profits during a recession.
16. How fifty-one-year-old Sheila C. accurately foresaw for the future a delightful, $20,000-a-year part-time self-employment career, for which she could prepare in her spare time.
17. How Hector K. grew rich easily by calculating his company's best business moves like a seer.

18. How Edward A. relieved his nagging headache with a simple thought.
19. How Alvin Z., who had trouble sleeping, slept at night like a log.
20. How middle-aged Jane L. stayed young despite her youth-robbing work.

You yourself can achieve what these people did—*and even more.* Let Frank Young teach you the different methods (scientifically refined) which these people used to attain their amazing successes. Trigger the secret mental power for each with the Miracle Mind Magic Stimulator *and make the seemingly impossible in your life come true.* You require no expensive equipment with possible side effects—no gadgets and no pills. You need *just yourself—and the easy secret trigger to detonate your dynamic physiological language swiftly.*

Contents

What This Book Can Do for You 7

    The Search for the Miracle Trigger   7

    The Secret of the Miracle Mind Magic Stimulator   8

Lesson 1   *How Your Secret Mental Powers Can Work*
                  Miracles for You 17

    How You, Too, Can Retire Much Earlier with Comparatively
        Little Capital—and Grow Rich Afterwards   18

    How You, Too, Can Know When to Step Out of a Successful
        Situation Before It Crashes, and Enter a New One and "Cash In"
        on It   20

    How You, Too, Can Save Yourself from Ruin by Recalling the
        "Important Forgotten Thing"   21

    How You, Too, Can Make Anybody Who Lords It Over You Look Up
        to You   22

Lesson 2   *The Basis of Your Secret Mental Powers* 24

    Why the Power of Your Conscious Mind is Tremendously
        Underrated   24

    Scientific Proof That Conscious-Mind Power is More Effective Than
        Hypnosis   25

    The Physiological Language of Your Mental Powers   27

    How the Conscious Mind Even Controls the Influence of Drugs on the
        Body   28

    The Tremendous Importance of the New Milieu   29

    How a Secret Mental Power Controls Your Nervous System   29

    How a Secret Mental Power Can Control Your Personality   30

    How a Secret Mental Power Can Control Your Physical Strength   31

    How a Secret Mental Power Can Control the Known and Unknown
        Secretions in Your Brain   32

    How a Secret Mental Power Can Control Your Body Tissues   33

    How a Secret Mental Power Can Control Your Vanishing Youth and
        Longevity   36

    How a Secret "Lazy" Mental Power Brings You a Power of Foresight
        That Makes You Unsurpassable   37

Lesson 2   The Basis of Your Secret Mental Powers, cont.

How a Secret Mental Power Can Control Your Natural Talents   38

Lesson 3   How to Unleash Your Secret Mental Powers. . . 40

Why You Don't Think with Your Brain Alone   40
Acquired Mental Distortions Which Limit Your Secret Mental Powers
    and How to Overcome Them   41
Acquired Physical Distortions Which Limit Your Secret Mental
    Powers   42
How the Curvature of Your Spine Can Increase—or Decrease the Dyna-
    mite of Your Secret Mental Powers   43
How to Release the Secret Mental Powers Strangled Within You by a
    Squeezing Spine   44
How a Secret Mental Power Can Heal Different Ailments Through Their
    Different Physiological Languages   44
How to Induce the Nerve Fibers of any Secret Mental Power to "Line
    Up Right" in Your Brain and Bring About the Miracle of Mind
    Magic   45
The Three Steps of the Miracle Mind Magic Stimulator to Trigger Your
    Secret Mental Powers   46
How to Practice Intensifying the Miracle Mind Magic
    Stimulator   47
The Secret of the Power of the Miracle Mind Magic
    Stimulator   48

*Lesson 4   How to Use Your Mental Power of Intellectual
                Leverage* *51*

The Amazing Profits from Using Intellectual Leverage   52
The Great Opportunities Missed from Lack of Intellectual
    Leverage   52
What Intellectual Leverage Is   53
Why You Lack Intellectual Leverage   53
How to Acquire Intellectual Leverage   54
How to Apply Intellectual Leverage on People   55
How to Amass Wealth with Intellectual Leverage   56
How to Apply Intellectual Leverage for Self-Defense   57
How to Apply Intellectual Leverage to Control Your Unhappy
    Moods   58
How to Trigger the Secret Mental Power of Intellectual Leverage with
    the Miracle Mind Magic Stimulator   59

Lesson 5   The Secret Mental Power to Overcome Your
*   Confused Thinking* *63*

How Confused Thinking Usually Starts   64
How to Overcome Confused Thinking   65
The Secret of Interesting Yourself in any Subject—Your Hidden Talent
        Opener   68
How to Resist Forming Confused Thinking About any New
        Knowledge   68
How to Trigger Overcoming and Preventing Confused Thinking with
        the Miracle Mind Magic Stimulator   69

Lesson 6   The Secret Mental Power of Psycho-Photographic
*   Memory* *73*

The Fantastic Profits from Developing a Psycho-Photographic
        Memory   74
The Nucleus of Psycho-Photographic Memory   74
Magic Aids for Acquiring Psycho-Photographic Memory Much
        Faster   77
Other Magic Aids for Acquiring Psycho-Photographic Memory Much
        Faster   79
The Serious Obstacles to Your Acquiring Psycho-Photographic
        Memory   80
How to Trigger Psycho-Photographic Memory in You with the Miracle
        Mind Magic Stimulator   80

Lesson 7   Secret Mental Powers for Profitable
*   Concentration* *85*

The Fantastic Profits from Using Profitable Concentration   85
How Unprofitably Your "Usual Self" Concentrates   86
How to Use Your Secret Power to Concentrate Profitably   87
The Sixteen Secret Rules for Profitable Concentration   88
The Seven Secret Rules for Profitable Concentration for Research,
        Which Brought Great Riches to Different People   90
How to Trigger Yourself to Concentrate Profitably with the
        Miracle Mind Magic Stimulator   91

Lesson 8   The Secret Mental Power to Control Your
*   Nervous Tension and Worry* *97*

Profits You Can Realize from Controlling Nervous Tension and
        Worry   98

*Lesson 8   The Secret Mental Power to Control Your
Nervous Tension and Worry, cont.*

What Happens in Your Body Due to Nervous Tension and
Worry   99
Why Your Physiological Language of Fear Soon Develops into an
Uncontrollable Habit   99
How Your Acquired Physiological Language of Fear Alters Your
Body Responses and Makes Those Changes Permanent   100
How You Regularly Reverse the Physiological Habit of Pain in
You   100
The Magic of the Psycho-Feedback: The Strictly Mental Alpha High
to Relax and Unwind You Anywhere, at any Time   101
How to Control Your Nervous Tension and Worry Immediately with
the Psycho-Feedback   102
How to Control Your Nervous Tension and Worry Swiftly with the
Psycho-Feedback   104
Why the Psycho-Feedback Gets Rid of Your Nervous Tension and
Worry Quickly and Effectively   105
The Miracle of the "Thought Beat"   105

*Lesson 9   The Secret Mental Power to Protect Yourself from
Domination by Others* *110*

Profits You Can Realize by Protecting Yourself from Domination
by Others   111
What Happens in Your Mind When You Are Dominated by
Someone   111
What Happens to Your Actions and Behavior When You Are
Dominated by Someone   112
What Happens to Your Physiological Language When You Are
Dominated by Someone   113
The Secret Clench-and-Relax to Protect You Against Being
Dominated by Others   113
The Clench-and-Relax Program   114

*Lesson 10   Your Secret Mental Power to Gain Swift Control
Over Others* *118*

The Fantastic Profits Gained from Swift Control Over Others   119
How Others Resist Your Efforts to Control Them   119
The Obstacles You Face in Trying to Control Others   120
How to Soften Someone's Resistance to Your Controlling Him
Swiftly   121

Lesson 10   Your Secret Mental Power to Gain Swift
               Control Over Others, cont.

How to Convert a Person into Your Physiologically-Synchronizing
     Twin   122
How to Condition Your Parasympathetic Nervous System   122
How to Trigger Your Control Over Others with the Miracle Mind
     Magic Stimulator   123
How to Proceed to Control Anyone   123

Lesson 11   Your Secret Mental Power to Enthrall Friends
               or Enemies 129

The Fantastic Profits from Enthralling Friends or Enemies   130
The Magic Difference in Your Life Resulting from Your Enthralling
     Even a Few Enemies   130
How to Prevent Anybody, Anywhere, from Disliking You at
     Sight   131
The Physiological Normalizing of Other People for Your Benefit   132
The Physiological Reversal to Stop People from Considering You as
     Being Ordinary   133
How to Be Above Being Considered Merely Ordinary   133
Why It Is Difficult to Understand Other People Quickly   134
How to Make Everybody Like You and Want to Know You by
     Using the Right Physiological Language   135
How to Avoid Unnecessary Losses   136
How to Trigger the Secret Mental Power to Enthrall Friend or
     Enemy with the Miracle Mind Magic Stimulator   137

Lesson 12   Your Secret Mental Power for Most Effective
               Judgment 141

The Fantastic Profits from Most Sensible Judgment   141
The Nine Main Causes That Hinder You from Arriving at the
     Most Sensible Judgment in Your Everyday Life   142
How to Trigger Your Most Sensible Judgment with the Miracle
     Mind Magic Stimulator   151
Your Personal Program   151

Lesson 13   Secret Mental Power for Wisest Future
               Action 155

The Fantastic Profits from Wisest Future Action   155

*Lesson 13   Secret Mental Power for Wisest Future
               Action, cont.*

How to Trigger Your Wisest Future Action with the Miracle Mind
    Magic Stimulator   170

*Lesson 14   The Secret Mental Power to Time Your Actions
               Perfectly* *176*

The Fantastic Profits from Timing Perfectly in Life   177
The Magic of Perfect Timing in Life   177
The Magic of Perfect Timing in Business   178
Ill-Timed, Shackling Introspection, and How to Prevent It from
    Ruining Your Opportunities   179
How to Oust the Crippling Physiological Language of Ill-Timed,
    Shackling Introspection   180
The Magical "Thought Plateau" to Lower the Blood Pressure of
    Your Crippled Physiological Language at Will   181
How to Trigger Perfect Timing with the Miracle Mind Magic
    Stimulator   182

*Lesson 15   Secret Mental Power to Route Your Nagging Aches
               and Minor Illness.* *187*

The Fantastic Profits from Routing Nagging Aches and Minor
    Illness   188
How Your Everyday Bad Habits Can Bring on Nagging Aches and
    Minor Illness   188
How Your Daily Unsuspected Bad Posture Can Bring on Nagging
    Aches and Minor Illness   189
How Your Common Dietary Habits Can Bring on Nagging Aches
    and Minor Illness   190
How Your Daily Tensions Can Bring on Nagging Pains and Minor
    Illness   191
How to Change Your Daily, Unsuspected Bad Posture That Brings
    on Nagging Pains and Minor Illness   192
The Simple Thought to Change Your Unsuspected Bad Posture
    That Brings on Nagging Pains and Minor Illness   192
How to Nullify Your Daily Tensions That Bring on Nagging Aches
    and Minor Illness   193
How to Trigger Routing Your Nagging Aches and Minor Illness
    with the Miracle Mind Magic Stimulator   194

Lesson 16   Secret Mental Power for Sexual Vitality 199

The Amazing Gains from Sexual Vitality and Marital Bliss   200
Why Your Domestic Familiarity Can Breed Marital Contempt   200
Why Decreased Sexual Vitality Can Endanger Your Marital
    Bliss   201
Why You Have to Add Ecstasy to Your Domestic Familiarity   201
How Your Usual Mental Attitude Bars Ecstasy from Your
    Domestic Familiarity   202
How to Overcome the Influence of Your Usual Mental Attitude
    Which Bars Ecstasy from Your Domestic Familiarity   203
How to Add Ecstasy to Your Domestic Familiarity   204
How to Trigger Sexual Vitality and Marital Bliss with the Miracle
    Mind Magic Stimulator   205

Lesson 17   How to Use Secret Mental Powers to Stay
                 Younger and Live Longer 209

The Fantastic Profits from Staying Young and Living Long   210
The Physiological Language That Keeps You Young   210
How Your Two Involuntary Nervous Systems May Fail to Keep
    You Speaking the Physiological Language of Youth   211
The Three Magic Secrets to Stay Young and Live Long with a
    Flexible Physiological Language   213
How to Trigger Your Staying Young and Living Long with the
    Miracle Mind Magic Stimulator   216
Your Personal Program   216

Lesson 18   Instant Physio-Magic: The Secret of Perpetual
                 Miracle Mind Magic 221

The Three Secret Steps of Instant Physio-Magic   221
The Magic Power of the Three Secret Steps to Get What You Want,
    for Nothing   222
The Miracle of Instant Physio-Magic   222
Step-by-Step Method for Using the New Miracle-Mind You   223

Brief Glossary of Terms 225

Lesson 1

How Your Secret Mental Powers Can Work Miracles for You

How Tim and Esther Were Able to Retire at Forty-five with $25,000, and at Sixty Were Worth $500,000

When he was a young man, Tim decided he wanted to retire early. He was industrious and willing to do his share of work, but he felt that at forty-five a man had done his full share and should be able to retire and enjoy himself while he was still young enough to do so. At forty, he didn't want to wait until he and Esther, his wife, were a "doddering old couple, with but a few more good years to live," as he acidly put it, before being able to see the whole world and do the things they had always yearned to do but never could, due to pressure of time, weariness after their full day's jobs, taking care of their two children, and the other duties of everyday living.

Tim prayed for the day when they could just lay around the beach or drift through the wide-open spaces with nothing on their minds. They had turned into working machines to raise and educate their two children, pay for their home, for their social security and pensions, and to save $15,000. At sixty-five they expected to retire and look and feel old, and probably die a few years later. Or they would be so accustomed to punching the time clock that they would go "crazy" and scramble back to any kind of work, just to keep busy and remain sane.

I met Tim at this time and he told me his problem. I taught him the secret mental power for wisest future action, and he mastered it promptly. In very short order he evolved a plan. It was a simple one. It consisted of buying stocks with most of the family savings, when they were down enough, and waiting patiently for them to rise to a satisfactory level before selling them. The whole cycle took place once or twice a year, on the average. Once he bought them, he forgot about them for months and enjoyed his regular life with his family and his work, the best he could. By the time he was forty-five, he had saved $25,000 and his children had finished college.

So Esther and he retired. Every year thereafter Tim invested more and more in such stocks, since he had more and more profits left. By the time he was sixty his holdings were worth about $500,000. At sixty-five he was on the way to becoming a millionaire. He and Esther are in fine health, look much younger than their years, are at peace, and are bursting with humor and good nature. They expect to live "a great many" more years and have seen the whole world "over and over." His monthly social security check is but a drop in the financial bucket to him, and he stopped long ago being a "work horse."

How You, Too, Can Retire Much Earlier with Comparatively Little Capital—and Grow Rich Afterwards

What Tim and Esther did, you can do, too. You don't have to retire if you don't want to lose your pension, but you can still start enjoying yourself much earlier than otherwise and grow rich while doing it. You don't have to follow Tim's system if you don't want to. Many people can't invest confidently in the stock market.

Another couple applied that same secret mental power and bought, instead, an apartment building, and paid off the mortgage from the rent. They, too, retired from their jobs at forty-five and lived off the rents. With simple tastes, they had all the free time they needed. Being mechanically inclined, the husband didn't mind doing some of the upkeep around the place several hours a day. The rest of the time he was "free as a lord." Once a year he arranged with the neighbor landlord to "take it over" for him, and he and his wife vacationed in exciting places out of season. Year after year goes by, and they look remarkably young. Their land, meanwhile, has risen so steadily in value that before long, they can sell it at a sky-high profit.

With the secret mental power for wisest future action, you, too, can select a practical road to early retirement which suits you most, and grow rich painlessly afterwards—and stay astonishingly young, calm, and contented for the rest of your life, never worrying about being a work horse indefinitely.

*How Fred Knew When to Step Out of a "Big
Business Thing" Before It Failed and Enter into a
New Thing in Time to "Cash In" on It*

Fred had looked for a long time for a "big thing" in which to invest his savings and time. He was sick and tired of just working for others and wanted to become independent, so he could live the luxurious life. Just to work for security for his wife and kids alone, he felt, was not enough. "You live just once," he told Joan, his wife. "If you don't enjoy it while you can, you never will."

"But how can you enjoy it in these days of inflation?" she asked him in despair. "The cost of living and taxes never stop rising! Even what you put in the bank, loses buying power every day! And things can't get better, the way they are going. We enjoy more luxuries only because we buy them on credit! We couldn't afford to buy them at all, otherwise! But then, we have to pay for them—with *interest!* That, too, raises the cost of living! After you retire, your pension, social security, and dividends will shrink in buying power, too, no matter what is done to try to make them bigger!"

"That's exactly what I mean!" Fred replied. "Either I find a way to make enough money while I'm still middle-aged, or I'll be working and paying through the nose all my life, and praying to end up well-off sometime before I die. I *have* to find a way to make big money *now* from a 'big thing,' or I will just waste my life away!"

With the secret mental power to time a deal perfectly, which I taught Fred, he found the "big thing" in which to invest his time and effort, and "struck it rich!" He couldn't believe there was so much money to be made, he confessed to me, although he and his family had to "pitch into it" for long hours every day. But after seven or eight years, he figured, he would be a millionaire! And he'd be only fifty! What a life he and the family could lead afterward!

Three years later I surprised Fred by urging him to apply, next, the secret mental power of wisest future action. Nothing in life, I insisted, turned out exactly as one planned.

With this next secret mental power he reluctantly listed the worst that could befall him in his prosperous enterprise, and prepared a list so he would not be caught by surprise. A few months later, the financial bottom fell out of the "big thing." But Fred had already invested in safe securities.

He bought now, however, into another "big thing" while the buying price was low, and it also started climbing fast. Fred plans to sell it in time, too, and retire altogether and enjoy the luxurious life.

How You, Too, Can Know When to Step Out of a Successful Situation Before It Crashes, and Enter a New One and "Cash In" on It

You, too, can do what Fred did and start enjoying the luxurious life while you still have some time to do it. Such opportunities exist all around you all the time. You may even recognize some of them, but a lot of other people also recognize them before long and pour into them. The price of the "big thing" zooms as a result, and you grow reckless and greedy to get rich with it. You then need the secret mental power of wisest future action, as given in this book, to help you determine when is the best time to "get out from under," before its financial structure starts falling and crushing you into bankruptcy under its weight. With your gains drawing dividends in safe securities, you can look around for another potential "big thing" and buy into it while it is ridiculously low-priced, and sell out again while the price is rising feverishly to phenomenal heights—or before the oncoming big crash! Do so a few times, and you can retire altogether and live the luxurious life surprisingly early!

How Ed Saved Himself from Legal Catastrophe by
Digging Out of His Mind the Important Minor
Evidence that Crushed His Enemies

Ed was in court, being unfairly prosecuted, he told me. The allegations against him were twisted around to mislead the court and brand him with a stigma that could ruin his future prospects. Yet, the misleading evidence being introduced supported it. His lawyer objected to it repeatedly, but had nothing forceful enough to hit back with. Exasperated, he put Ed on the stand and brought out some salient points in his favor, but the mountain of misleading evidence against him was overwhelming. Ed knew he was innocent, but could not prove it.

He came to me that night in a frenzy. I taught him the secret mental power of *intellectual leverage.* He hurried home and practiced it, and applied it as he lay in bed. An hour later he dug out of his mind an important piece of evidence that he had forgotten. Next morning he confided it to his lawyer. His lawyer "pumped" him about it.

In court that morning, Ed's lawyer let the opposition empty its arsenal. Then, suddenly, he brought in the evidence Ed was able to recall. It went off like a bomb. The oppositon gave up. Ed had saved himself from a legal catastrophe.

How You, Too, Can Save Yourself from Ruin by Recalling the "Important Forgotten Thing"

In a lawsuit or in any other challenge in life, you frequently face disaster just because you can't recall the little "forgotten thing." It is not something you have memorized and forgotten, as you did in school, but something to which you paid little attention when it occurred, or which you considered too unimportant at the time. Even if it is lodged in your subconscious mind, you cannot dig it out easily because you don't know what you want. You have to *think* it out! Your subconscious is not a god to serve you.

With the secret mental power of *intellectual leverage,* you can provide your *conscious mind* with the "mental triggering device" it needs to think out the "forgotten thing" with cold logic, and enable you to catch your rivals by surprise and crush them.

*How Larry Made Those Who Lorded It Over Him
Look Up to Him in Admiration*

There was nothing exceptional about Larry, and hardly anybody gave him a second look. This feeling of universal unimportance crushed his spirits and made him still less in the eyes of others. When he tried to call attention to himself, by speaking loud or moving about importantly, he stirred amusement or drew mockery from others. He was praised only for being hard-working and conscientious, and was tolerated like a mongrel acting like a pedigreed watchdog. Larry was so infuriated by it all that he grew deeply resentful of everybody and attracted the wrong kind of attention to himself.

He confessed his problem to me, and I taught him the secret mental power to bring him *swift control over others.* Larry listened carefully. First, he learned how others would resist his efforts to control them. Second, he found out what obstacles he would face when trying to control them, and how their resistance to him would increase. He practiced and mastered that secret mental power, and how to make others *think his physiological language* to his benefit.

Next day, he tackled the same people he had failed to impress and, to his amazement, controlled them swiftly! His social success took a big leap forward, and he was soon in line for a big raise and an unbelievable promotion *at a time when others were being laid off!*

How You, Too, Can Make Anybody Who Lords
It Over You Look Up to You

You, too, can stop taking a back seat in life and letting others lord it over you. You can stop being squashed under their social hauteur just because you aren't imposing-looking or hold no important position. Such people make you feel like a nobody and keep you secretly angry, resentful, dissatisfied, and despising yourself. You become humorless, antisocial, petulant, and sarcastic, and end up a laughingstock. "That hopeless person!" they smirk about you among themselves. You feel as if life is not worth living, and hate the day you were born. You waste a lot of precious time comparing yourself to others, always to your own disadvantage. *Everybody*, you think to yourself, has more of everything than you do. You envy their financial status, their social positions, their occupational standings, their appearances, their wives, their children, their friends, their homes, their cars, their clothes. You envy them until your face burns with fury. You are dying to make others admire you as *you* admire them.

That's what Larry did with the secret mental power of *intellectual leverage*. He made others stop lording it over him and admire *him* instead.

These are only samples of the numerous case histories you will find in this book, of people who have used one secret mental power after another to achieve seemingly impossible goals. Apply the programs in this book to trigger these powers with the Miracle Mind Magic Stimulator, and you will swiftly acquire the stunning power of the miracle of mind magic.

Lesson 2

The Basis of Your
Secret Mental Powers

Why the Power of Your Conscious Mind Is
Tremendously Underrated

So much emphasis has been placed on the power of the *subconscious* mind and on *psychic* power that the power of the *conscious* mind has become tremendously underrated. In fact, many of the most staggering performances of the subconscious mind or of psychic powers are actually *conscious-mind powers*! But they are so incredible that they have not been considered as stemming from the conscious mind. The division between the conscious mind, the subconscious mind, and the psychic power mind, however, is hard to draw, and incredible mental achievements are accomplished as easily through the conscious mind as through any other mind. Even *more incredible ones*, indeed, because, with the conscious mind, *you, yourself, are totally in control of everything you do*!

You are not lying helpless in a trance or in some other vague state, but are *fully alive* and *thoroughly aware* of *every move you make*! You are in a state in which you can make up your mind, or change it, *the very instant you experience anything*. You don't have to wait until you wake up or regain your conscious self to analyze what took place. You are *always* the "superman" then, not just when in a psychic trance, or in a dreamy state, or when shackled in a chair to a brain-wave device. In that way you can develop *increasing conscious-mind power*, like the athlete who gets stronger the more he exercises. You thereby *become* a different and more effective person *all the time*, and remain one! Harvard psychologist, Dr. Robert Rosenthal, showed that when teachers were misled into thinking they were teaching a class of geniuses (by presenting them with false I.Q. scores), the teacher responded by teaching the children as if they *had* a classful of geniuses. The same children, it turned out, registered an average of twenty-five points higher in their I.Q.'s! Through their conscious-mind efforts, in other words, the students increased their intelligences by one-quarter—or entered from the average-minded into the *genius class*! Their achievements in life thereafter shifted from that of the average mind into that of a "genius." They had become "geniuses" with their *conscious minds*—and could remain "geniuses" if they wished! They didn't have to fall into trances first! *Your own conscious mind can do that for you with any mental power you wish!*

Scientific Proof That Conscious-Mind Power Is More Effective Than Hypnosis

Psychologists have found that amazing feats performed under hypnosis, like turning into a "human plank"; withstanding seemingly excruciating pain; lifting staggering weights; locking the hands together like two pieces of welded steel, so that the harder you try to tear them apart, the more strongly they lock together; displaying fantastic endurance, and so on, can be done with the conscious mind *without* falling into the hypnotic trance. Behavior under the hypnotic trance, they conclude, is more easily explained, therefore, as caused by *a change in the subject's attitudes, expectancies, and willingness to cooperate with the directions given him!*

Several hundred investigators have made such findings during recent years. Dr. Barber (at the Medfield Foundation) showed that four out of every five individuals can normally suspend themselves between two chairs when simply *asked* to make their bodies rigid. Dr. Collins (from Australia) demonstrated that the average man or woman can remain thus suspended up to four minutes. No attempt was even *made* to hypnotize these persons, and they were bewildered by their own powers. Dr. Orne (Harvard) showed that *nonhypnotized* men showed much greater strength and endurance than normal when *wide awake* but *properly motivated*. At the Medfield Foundation, it was proved that pain could be reduced by suggestions, regardless of whether or not the subject was hypnotized. My own uncle had a deep, triple-rooted third molar extracted without anesthesia, simply by gripping the handles of the dental chair with all his might. And he did not let out a sound. Dr. Barber concluded that distraction was more effective than hypnosis in reducing pain.

Other experiments conducted at the Foundation proved that many people were *more highly responsive* to suggestions when *not* hypnotized and when merely told to *imagine* that their hands were so firmly locked together, for instance, that they could *not* draw them apart; or when merely told that they could *not* rise from their chairs, or speak their own names, or forget certain "things" they had heard or seen. At least twenty percent of them passed *all* such tests and confessed that they actually *felt* the things suggested.

The Motivation Key

Some scientists, it is true, have noted that the subjects *do show* a small increase in suggestibility following hypnosis, but that it is missed because it is so small. Their explanation is that the hypnotists make certain that their subjects are motivated to do their best, and that such instructions *alone* raise a subject's suggestibility above his normal level. The hypnotist is motivating the subject to do something he has never done before. He fills him with the confidence necessary to perform the feat; he assures him that it will be safe, and that he can perform it if only he tries. The *confidence* which he pumps into the subject, these scientists conclude, is the key to the hypnotic performance.

Other scientists have even failed to detect any difference between the hypnotic trance and the wide awake state. The subject may think he is in a trance, in other words, because he has been *told* so by the hypnotist. No physiological changes, however, have been demonstrable between the normal state and "trance" state.

Their conclusion is that hypnotism is neither special nor mysterious, and that *your own potential* is simply *much greater* than you have been led to believe. Your conscious mind, to state it simply, can do *anything* your subconscious mind can do under hypnosis.

Illusion

Illusions fall under the same principle. Psychologists now consider illusion merely one aspect of perception. If you present to your mind an *adequate* picture or some other kind of data, your brain will perceive the picture or data correctly. But if you present it with a *confusing* picture or data, your brain *won't* be able to come to a conclusion about it. The result is an *illusion*, for people trust what they see more than what they feel. There is evidence, too, that you tend to see some illusions according to how you think of yourself. (That's why you can't afford to let others lord it over you.)

In each and every case, it is your *conscious mind* which is working, and it can do for you *anything* which you can do with hypnosis. Even *more* so, because, when you depend upon hypnosis primarily, your conscious mind (your power of self-command) becomes weaker and weaker the more you depend upon the hypnotic state. While, when you depend upon your conscious mind alone, your conscious mind *grows stronger and stronger* the more you depend upon it, just as a muscle does the more you use it.

The Physiological Language of Your Mental Powers

How, you ask yourself now, can your conscious mind convert you from an average person into a genius in anything so easily? (Genius in anything means that you can be a genius or a superman not only academically, but also socially, in business, in your career, in controlling others, in keeping young and healthy, and living long—in short, in anything and everything you do.) Your conscious mind converts you into a genius simply with its own power. The students in the Rosenthal experiments did not purposely use the power of their conscious minds to convert themselves from average students into geniuses. They merely listened to the teacher—something they had regularly done before—but this time their *motivation* and their *enthusiasm* zoomed to such unusual heights that their whole bodies changed with them and "spoke" the *physiological language* of their feverishly stimulated minds. The quickened thinking which seized them from the teacher's new approach flooded their bodies with brain messages, through their nervous systems, and started their "tissue wheels" turning at a different speed. Every organ, every cell, their very blood circulation—in fact, *everything* in their bodies—fell into step with the "new persons" they had become and spoke a new *physiological language.*

Every student had become as different from what he had been before as the resting track star does when he dashes into action. His whole body now spoke a physiological language in tune with his mental powers. And he could halt that physiological language and resume it *at will* whenever he wished to, and without hypnosis, drugs, brain-wave devices, or any other artificial means with possible side effects.

How the Conscious Mind Even Controls the Influence of Drugs on the Body

Even when one takes drugs, they can influence him only according to his conscious mind's acceptance of them. That's why medical scientists have concluded that, no matter how specific the nervous and physiological effects of a drug may be, its psychological effects are exceedingly variable. Drugs alone, they insist, do *not* bring about in you such specific states as anger, depression, joy, and the like. Specificity of psychological effect *hardly ever comes* from the drug itself. It comes, rather, from the background or environment of the person taking it! A drug *does* introduce specific changes in one's body physiology, but these changes *do not* set off specific or uniform psychological behavior in him. It is his *surrounding social and environmental cues*, as well as his *past experiences with that drug*, which do it. The popularity of so many over-the-counter sedatives and tranquilizers, the researchers insist, could be mainly due to the ease with which drowsiness, lassitude, and general slowing of the body machinery could be *interpreted* as constituting "peace of mind." Even the sexual arousal quality of the "Spanish fly," these authorities add, may be confused with the fact that the drug irritates the urinary tract and thereby fools one into believing that his sexual apparatus is excited directly by it, instead of reflexly from the irritation.

The Tremendous Importance of the New Milieu

The new physiological language, which your conscious mind brings you when you change in any way, is most important to you because your "new brain" then has to live in your "new body" in order for you to use its new mental powers. Your "new brain" cannot use its new mental powers otherwise, no more than the sprinter can dash down the track with his heart, respiration, and sugar metabolism, to supply his now-active muscles, no different than while he was resting.

Experiments have show that using your brain is more fatiguing than using your muscles. That's why the thinker needs more sleep than the nonthinker. The physiological language of your body, therefore, *has* to change when the full power of your conscious mind is used. It has to change, in addition, because your "new brain" needs a *different milieu* or center of forces to operate in; a milieu of tissue that is metabolizing on the same physiological level as yourself! Without this new physiological language to operate with, your "new brain" will become your "old brain" once more. In this *new* milieu, however, it will explode with the dynamite of its secret mental powers, which it ordinarily does only when under the artificial influence of hypnosis, drugs, psychic power reveries, and so forth. With this new physiological language (which you will be taught how to trigger at will in the next lesson with the Miracle Mind Magic Stimulator), the incomparable power of your conscious mind can promptly bring you the power of a genius *in any field of endeavor.*

How a Secret Mental Power Controls Your Nervous System

With the different mental powers of your *conscious mind,* when you raise them from those of an ordinary person to those of a genius, you can achieve, with ease, one great wish after another and make your every dream come true *consciously*. You don't have to wait for a genie or some other "miracle," like your subconscious mind, psychic power, hypnosis, or some artificial mechanical device to shock you into it. You can do it yourself *any time, at will*! One of the most important secret mental powers you will acquire is the control over your nervous system. With it you can annihilate bad habits *in an instant*! You can alter your personality from the one you deplore into the one you wish you had—*in an instant*! You can banish nervous tension in an instant. You can master your temper, your lack of confidence, your tendency to cave in under stress, in an instant. You can end your tendency to exaggerate (in your imagination) the possible catastrophes that could befall you in anything you attempt, *in an instant*.

You have two important, but oppositely acting, involuntary nervous systems in your body. One is your parasympathetic. It keeps your natural functions normal: those of your appetite, your digestion, your metabolism, and those of your heart, liver, kidneys, and other organs. The other involuntary nervous system is your sympathetic (your nerves for meeting emergencies). It controls the power of your muscles and stimulates your heart, liver, and other organs to accelerate their functions, to provide your muscles with more blood and more blood sugar to enable them to fight against, or flee from, any danger. If the danger is mental, like the danger you encounter in any kind of competition (even in business or socially), your sympathetic nervous system provides you with the glandular secretions necessary to "sharpen up" your wits to meet it.

With a secret mental power, you can control these two nervous systems at will and improve your health, your digestion, and your feeling of well-being to the peak, or stimulate your brain like that of a genius or super-genius and achieve whatever goals you wish.

How a Secret Mental Power Can Control Your Personality

Behavior therapy was at first called "surface stuff" by psychiatrists, and was looked upon with benevolent amusement. But it is now agreed that if the personality is a person's "totality of habits and behavior," the elimination of his neurotic habits constitute, in itself, a kind of personality change. Even phobias are now being treated with techniques involving deep muscle relaxation. Since anxiety causes the muscles to tense and contract, relaxing the muscles causes the anxiety to vanish.

With a secret mental power, you can alter your whole personality because, with it, you can alter your whole behavior. Alter your personality first, by thinking of yourself as possessing a different personality than you have. That, in itself, alters your thinking, for you will then think as if you *did* possess that different personality. That carries over into your mental and physical behavior, and alters your physiological language to conform with your new personality. Your heart will beat like that of your new personality; your digestion will attune to it, as will your blood circulation and your metabolism. You *become* that new personality *all the way through you!*

How a Secret Mental Power Can Control Your Physical Strength

Just the same as you can alter your mental power from that of an ordinary person into that of a genius, *consciously and quickly* you can alter it from that of an ordinary person into that of a Hercules.

A man in a raging temper can hit three times as hard with his fist, or can lift something twice as heavy or more, than he can when he is in a normal frame of mind. At such times you are suddenly converted into *super-prime* physical shape; your adrenal glands flood your bloodstream with adrenalin and multiply your muscle tension to peak levels. Normally, you respond to a situation in a fraction of a second. But when swift reactions are needed, your brain reduces your reaction time to a millisecond. When faced with an ordeal, your body can consciously summon the most spectacular powers to its aid instantly.

Authorities agree, though, that more important than your physical powers for survival is the mental outlook which you acquire in times of trouble. (The *secret* mental power which you acquire then, in other words.) Stefansson, an expert on survival, says that during dangerous stress, a man who should be technically dead stays alive because he can use his physiological capacity to the full. All he needs, Stefansson adds, is a firm belief that he will survive, "and he probably will!" (Again, because of a secret mental power.)

Emotional Triggers Not Necessary

And you don't need fear or anger to trigger that secret mental power, either, according to Dr. Whitney. There is a pretty good chance that you have more strength than you imagine, he states, and certainly more than you use. The secret behind confounding feats of strength, he believes, depend upon your ability to increase your adrenalin release (through commanding your sympathetics), and to control your muscle fibers, at will. This is achieved through a secret mental power which swiftly triggers a revolutionary change in your physiological language.

All this is possible because your muscles are also directly under the control of your conscious mind through your pyramidal nervous system. This nervous system controls your *voluntary* muscles (that is, your skeletal muscles: your arm muscles, your leg muscles, your chest muscles, your back muscles), as distinguished from your *in*voluntary muscles (the muscles of your stomach, arteries, bronchi, urinary bladder, all of which are controlled by your parasympathetics or sympathetics, or both). Your pyramidal nervous system also fills your muscles with muscle tone, causing them to contract much harder. Your subconscious mind, too, automatically commands your sympathetics to stimulate your adrenal glands to secrete more and alter your physiological langauge to conform to that of a strong man in action. Without that necessary milieu, your muscles cannot contract their hardest nor remain super-powerful for very long. With a secret mental power, you can trigger all these super-power changes in you speedily, and maintain them with the right physiological language.

How a Secret Mental Power Can Control the Known and Unknown Secretions in Your Brain

The number of known chemical secretions in your brain continues to grow rapidly. All of them have specific effects on you. They are discharged automatically in your brain all day and night, according to how you think, act, and live. Science might never discover them all, for so many of them are secreted in different proportions (or perhaps even in different combinations) by different individuals. Some secretions alert you; others make you think faster or slower; others let you remember better or forget easier (an intolerable situation, for example); others tone up your nervous systems, and others relax them. The list of all they can do will never be complete.

The important thing is that your brain is not just a thinking tissue, but a secreter of different chemical substances as well. And its different secretions differ widely according to how your brain reacts to your body physiology and to your environment. What chemicals your brain secretes to adjust you to all the varying stresses of life is a secondary matter. More important is the fact that it *does* secrete innumerable different substances. It secretes them because your body has to *keep up* with varying stresses by regularly adjusting its physiological language to them, or by altering it to overcome them. Your subconscious mind will encourage your brain to secrete different chemical substances, too. But, frequently, these will be the *wrong kind* of secretions. A dread of something, which is suppressed in your subconscious mind, for instance, will automatically secrete in your brain the chemical related to that dread and alter your physiological language to flee from that situation whenever you face it again, instead of stimulating you to face it and figure out how to vanquish it with a secret mental power. With your *conscious mind*, however, you can *nullify* this unwanted secretion of your subconscious mind. And with a secret mental power you can secrete the *right* chemical in your brain to bring back the *right* physiological language to your body, so that you can solve and overcome the dreadful situation. Your conscious mind is, consequently, an absolutely necessary overseer for all your other minds, for it can keep your physiological language regularly at the tissue level of that of the "genius."

How a Secret Mental Power Can Control Your Body Tissues

The power of the conscious mind—even that of ordinary thinking—over the tissues is so phenomenal that even the most primitive creatures or structures alter their outer aspects by beautifying themselves in order to attract the opposite sex at mating time; such as, by acquiring dazzling plumes, or different colors to their hair or fur, or by growing adornments, like the cock's comb, the lion's mane, and so on.

Negatively, the power of the conscious mind can also *destroy* healthy tissues. Among the long-time scientifically accepted medical causes of ulcers are psychic causes, like worry, nervous tension, anxiety, and chronic fear. The mind, it is believed, in some way causes the ulcer to form, due to the physiological effects upon it of the psychic cause. The reason for that is unknown. The explanation, though, is probably the fact that when the mind is in the grip of any fear (including worry, which is usually saturated with fear), the sympathetic nervous system is constantly being stimulated by it to prepare it to fight or flee from the stimulation. The sympathetics, as a consequence, constrict the capillaries in the stomach to let more blood flow into the skeletal muscles and supply them with the necessary extra nutrition (sugar) they will need to meet the emergency. When, as a result of prolonged worry, the stomach is deprived for long periods of its normal supply of blood, its mucous membrane suffers from lack of enough nutrition and waste product removal, and ulcerates. Herpes simplex and other conditions attributed to psychic causes are apparently formed in a similar manner. Dr. Jonas Salk, developer of the polio vaccine, believes that emotional factors play a part in the development and spread of cancer, indirectly bringing it about through influencing its hormone system.

Take another example. You can improve your sight by simply *wanting* to! Show a woman a picture of a baby, and the pupils of her eyes will widen by twenty percent. Show a man the same picture and his eyes will not react, unless it happens to be his own child. But show him the picture of a good-looking girl and his eyes will open twenty percent wider than usual.

Take still another example. Up to seventy-five percent of the pain in a tense person disappears when he relaxes. Tension speeds up the blood circulation, and that increases the pressure on the nerves of pain. For that reason, the less highly strung you are, the less pain you will feel.

Why Your Conscious Mind Controls the State of Your Body Organs and Tissues

That is why your conscious mind controls the state of your tissues. It does so primarily through controlling the circulation of your blood going through them. People have turned gray overnight from excessive worry or great fright. Barney Ross, the famous boxer, turned gray in twenty-fours during World War II while cornered in a trench, from which he shot and killed twenty-three Germans before morning. There are cases in which an individual's leg shrank one whole inch in length overnight, from ghastly mental terror. Other people have even died from a great fright. In each and every case, the *conscious mind made the body speak a negative physiological language.*

In the same way, your conscious mind can control your tissues for their *improvement*. It does so with a secret mental power which makes them speak the *right* physiological language. Just as psychic reasons can cause ulcers, psychiatry may heal such ulcers by making the mind command the body to speak the right physiological language. It is commonly known among physicians that a secret mental power may heal warts. Secret mental powers have even overcome severe strokes that left the victim paralyzed from the neck down. This was the well-known case of Sir Winston Churchill, at age ninety-one.

It is equally well known that a physician may fail to heal a particular patient with all the skill he possesses, and then suddenly heal him by prescribing to him placebos (sugar-coated, medically inactive substances which pass for pills), which the patient is made to believe are curative pills. Indeed, latest medical statistics reveal that for every ten patients who benefit from the most modern drugs and antibiotics, one of them enjoys an effective and sometimes permanent cure by taking pills made entirely of sugar and water (placebos). In many instances, even an injection of distilled water may produce the same effect as an ampule of morphine.

Conscious Mind—The Healing Agent

In all these cases the healing agent was the *conscious mind*, for no attempt was made to hypnotize the patient. Nor did the patient resort to his psychic powers, to his subconscious mind, or to a brain-wave device. He was told that the thing or the thought given him would cure him, and it did. A leading neurologist insists that by *just assuring* the patient that his recurring headaches were not produced by a brain tumor was enough to clear them up. The cause of many headaches, he insists, are due to the patients' fears that they have some underlying brain disease. You can use that same secret mental power positively and fill yourself with superb health.

How a Secret Mental Power Can Control Your Vanishing Youth and Longevity

By habitually reminding yourself that you are getting older and older, as most people do, particularly when a new birthday reminds you of how "old" you are getting, you form a reminder of approaching old age in the brain cells of your subconscious mind which chronically keep your tissues oriented along that line. You become like the person who refused to believe that he was cured of a certain disease, and who therefore continued to "go downhill" and suffer from that disease, as if he still had it, even though the most thorough diagnosis revealed no remaining symptoms of it in him. That person had "tainted" his body cells with the effects of that disease. Even though he was no longer afflicted by it, his body cells were already acquainted with the effects of it and automatically continued to function as if he *still* had it. Or, like the woman who still believes she is homely after her features have been remodelled into those of a beauty. Her physiological language, as a result, still speaks as before, and she remains just as unhappy.

By reminding yourself continually that you are getting old and inlaying this habit in your subconscious mind, you oust all thoughts of youth from your brain and resign yourself to your fate. That accelerates the aging process.

With a secret mental power you will block this feeling of "inevitable old age" from your mind, even if you have to delude yourself and others that you are far from being "that old." That, in turn, fills your subconscious mind with that "younger" frame of mind, and your tissues react accordingly physiologically and start speaking the physiological language of continuing youth.

Many people unsuspectingly prolong their own lives with mental power, for there is a significant dip in death rates just before patients' birthdays, just before such major events as Presidential elections, and among Jewish patients just before the Day of Atonement. John Adams and Thomas Jefferson both lived until the fiftieth anniversary of the signing of the Declaration of Independence, and died that very afternoon. Trigger this right physiological language into your tissues regularly with the Miracle Mind Magic Stimulator, and you will become "young again" and stay so, seemingly endlessly.

How a Secret "Lazy" Mental Power Brings You a Power of Foresight That Makes You Unsurpassable

There is a secret "lazy" mental power that can bring you a power of foresight that makes you unsurpassable in *anything* you do. This secret "lazy" power is nothing else but the act of daydreaming. A substantial body of medical opinion is now convinced that daydreaming is by no means the trait of the lazy and absent-minded. On the contrary, it is now called one of the most valuable traits your conscious mind possesses. You can use its power to create "constructive fantasies," as the scientists term it, to tremendous advantage in your everyday life. Daydreams enable you, these authorities state, to try things out in fantasy before you attempt them in fact—somewhat like practice in athletics or rehearsal in dramatics. Daydreams enable you to "get out of yourself" and look at things from another point of view—from a more objective point of view. You can then see yourself as others see you—and can change yourself for the better before they see you again, and make them see you thereafter as you *want* them to see you.

With daydreaming, indulged in fully by your conscious mind, you can train your subconscious mind to react as *you* want it to react and use it to *reinforce* your conscious mind in meeting the obstacles you face. With it you can also figure out how best to meet any situation in life and force your conscious mind to prepare you effectively for it, and automatically trigger the right physiological language in you to perform it.

How a Secret Mental Power Can Control Your
Natural Talents

As stated before, when you lift yourself from the ordinary
person into the genius class, not only academically, but in
anything you do, your physiological language alters into that of
the superior person you have suddenly become. But already, as an
average person—

- You can run your hand across a smooth surface and detect
  projections only 1/25,000 of an inch high.
- You can taste one part of quinine in two million parts of
  water.
- You can detect between 2,000 and 10,000 different
  smells.
- You can store two and a half times more information than
  the world's most advanced computer.
- You have enough knowledge of one sort or another in
  your head to fill five million books.
- You have powers of calculation five times greater than the
  most advanced computer.
- Your brain contains between ten and fifteen billion
  separate nerve cells or neurons, or just about five times the
  present population of the world. The brain of a bee has
  only 900 cells, and that of an ant, 250 cells.

What Makes a Genius

Medical science already admits that there is hardly any
technical difference between your brain and, let's say, that of the
late Albert Einstein. The only difference (unless you are not a
natural genius) lies in the as yet unrecorded codes through which
the messages to your brain are passed up the vital cable of nerves
within your spinal cord. This code, scientists feel, directs blood to
your brain coverings (your meninges), and strengthens and
invigorates the central supervisory organ of your nervous system.
This "supervisory organ" determines how hard your brain will
work.

A secret mental power can direct this supervisory organ to
work for you *consciously* at full blast. In men of genius, the brain

membranes are richer in blood vessels. Their brains, as a result, are richly supplied with blood and oxygen. Your brain needs oxygen very badly because your spinal cord buzzes constantly with electrical nerve impulses (like the dots and dashes of the Morse code), as it carries a two-way flow of information between your body and your brain.

How to Control Nervous Tension

Even nervous tension, which emanates from the frontal lobes of your brain, can distort or block these messages. Fresh air and good posture are of paramount importance for the proper functioning of your brain because they bring more oxygen into your nervous system and keep your spinal cord "straight," so the two-way flow of electrical nerve impulses through it can proceed without interruption. This vital supply of oxygen to your brain can be advantageously increased with a secret mental power which stimulates your sympathetics, for these dilate the blood vessels of your brain. Oxygen intake is so urgently necessary for your possessing a brain like a "genius," researchers found, that when they restricted the oxygen intake of a group of volunteers in I.Q. tests, their performances plunged sharply downward. The moment the oxygen intake was restored to normal, their performances improved decidedly. (That's why people with above-average lung capacity have a correspondingly greater chance of being mentally above average.) "Using" your brain *at a certain time* every day, and at a particular place, the scientists discovered, conditions it to work harder and better with the least driving effort. With a secret mental power, you can trigger your brain to its full working capacity with the Miracle Mind Magic Stimulator any time of day, anywhere. Besides, you can do it *consciously!*

How to Trigger Your Natural Talents

So, proceed now and develop your secret mental powers, control your natural talents *all the time*, and achieve the seemingly incredible *any time you wish*, simply by triggering your Miracle Mind Magic Stimulator. Master this great "genius-bringing" skill in the next lesson and use it with *every* secret mental power.

Lesson 3

How to Unleash Your
Secret Mental Powers

Why You Don't Think with Your Brain Alone

When you think, your brain alone does *not* do the thinking. Your body thinks along with it, by instantly responding to it. Your nerve centers think, too. Among these are:

- Your nerve ganglia (the aggregation of nerve cells along your sensory nerves—or of the nerves which carry the messages *from* your body *to* your brain)
- Your nerve plexuses (the networks or interjoinings of your nerves)
- Your nerve reflexes (the reactions of your nerves to stimulation)

All this is part of the new physiological language which your body speaks when you think, most of which is invisible to yourself and others, except when you turn pale, blush or flush, tremble, your eyes shine, you become restless, pugnacious, or burst into flight. You, like fifteen percent of people, might even have a fantasy-making mechanism built into your mind, scientists have proved, and might even "hear" colors as well as sounds and words when you think. That would alter your physiological language still more. Tension on your spinal cord through wrong posture would also affect the two-way flow of nerve-electricity passing up and down between your body and your brain. The state of tension or relaxation of your skeletal muscles when you think will also affect your thoughts, either through your muscles "thinking with" them by your automatically assuming postures or movements suggestive of their success, or by their "thinking against" them by your automatically assuming postures or movements suggestive of their failure. Even the presence or absence of pain (like a headache or stomachache) will encourage your body organs to, or discourage them from "thinking along" with you, and thereby also affect the resulting physiological language which your thoughts trigger in you.

When you think seriously, then, it is best if you can do so under favorable circumstances, for it takes very little to disrupt the smooth stream of the two-way flow of the information whizzing up and down your spinal cord. Brain-work, it is also essential to realize (as has been suggested before), is nearly twice as tiring as manual labor. When you work with your brain you need more sleep and rest than when you work with muscle "alone." It takes only about four hours sleep to restore your physical energy, scientists have proven in the laboratory, but nearly twice as long to recover from brain fatigue. And when your brain is fatigued you think with weary organs, soaked with body wastes and starved of oxygen. Unless you are in an emergency, it is wisest to be rested before you trigger and use a secret mental power, if you expect the best results for your effort.

Acquired Mental Distortions Which Limit Your Secret Mental Powers and How to Overcome Them

Any mental distortion which makes you feel inferior to others or to any situation, will limit your mental powers. If you worry about the shape of your nose, the width of your shoulders (if you are a man), the height of your breasts (if you are a woman), the size of your waistline, your loss of youth, the amount of your income, your lack of importance where you work, the possibility of your not being secure enough in your old age, your diminishing sexual potency, the uncertainties of the stock market, the fidelity of your marriage partner, your children's behavior in school or college, your having to start a new career in middle age, or whatever else that frustrates you, you will deplete the natural nerve-electricity potential in your brain and nervous systems, and lessen the dynamite behind your secret mental powers by altering your physiological language *negatively*. It is not the momentary worrying that depletes your natural nerve-electricity potential, but the habit of constant fretting over one thing after another which it launches.

The quick way to end worry and stop depleting your natural nerve-electricity potential is to think of something else at once—something you enjoy and which took place already. Think of some sport event, for instance, in which the team or athlete you favored won spectacularly, and relive the contest in your conscious mind. Think of a vacation in which you had a whale of a good time. Think of someone you met whose company you relished no end. Even play solitaire, if you delight in that. "Flee" from the intolerable situation of the present, in other words, by "daydreaming" productively about the past. When your mind is rested and you have regained your normal nerve-electricity potential, again tackle the problem that bothers you, and trigger the secret mental power necessary to solve it with the Miracle Mind Magic Stimulator, and annihilate the problem.

Acquired Physical Distortions Which Limit Your Secret Mental Powers

The most important physical distortion which limits your secret mental powers is an abnormal spinal curvature. Your spine extends from the base of your skull all the way down to your hipbones, and it houses most of your spinal cord. Your spinal cord consists of all the nerves that pass down *from* your brain *to* your body, and of those that pass up *from* your *body to* your brain, except those which pass from your brain to your face. It extends from the base of your skull to the tip of your sacrum. A physical distortion of your spinal cord may commence from as far up as inside your skull, and continue beyond where the nerves passing through it exit from your spine and sacrum into your body. Its effects may be felt, through nerve radiation, all the way from some nerve center in your brain to the ending of that nerve somewhere in your body.

There are other physical distortions which also limit your secret mental powers, particularly because they either cause or add to your abnormal spinal curvature; such as, round or uneven shoulders, carrying the head too far forward or backward, walking with one or both feet thrown outward instead of pointing directly ahead, engaging in sports or occupations which regularly compel you to assume bad posture for long periods of time, or a sagging abdomen which drags your rib cage downward. (Such conditions and their serious anatomical and physiological effects on you mentally and physically are described fully in my book, *Yoga for Men Only*, (Parker Publishing Co.) should you be interested in studying them in detail. But that is not necessary here.) Physical distortions resulting from pain from any ailment will also limit your secret mental powers. Pain distracts from full mental concentration, and it also usually forces you to alter your normal posture and movements to ease it. Your spine has to accommodate for that resulting imbalance in your body mechanics by assuming one or more abnormal curves, thereby throwing tension on your spinal cord.

How the Curvature of Your Spine Can Increase—or Decrease—the Dynamite of Your Secret Mental Powers

The curvature of your spine can increase or decrease the dynamite of your secret mental powers because, as already stated, the nerve-electricity potential in your brain and nervous systems flows two ways through your spinal cord. When any part of your spinal cord is twisted or compressed, or impinged by the walls of your spine, the nerves on that side of your spinal cord are numbed to a variable degree and restrict the easy flow of nerve-electricity through them. The nerves on the *other side* of that same part of your spinal cord, on the other hand, may be abnormally stretched or twisted by your abnormal spinal curvature because your spinal cord is then twisted also, since it is closely housed by your spine. Such an abnormal tension on that whole part of your spinal cord exhausts the nerves passing through it and reduces their efficiency to transmit the full voltage of the nerve-electricity flowing the two ways through them.

When your spinal distortion is of long duration, permanent changes may have taken place in the discs between the vertebrae and impinge upon the nerves of your spinal cord reducing the voltage of the nerve-electricity flowing up and down the spinal cord. When the spinal distortion is lessened, your spinal cord will regain some of its lost voltage of nerve-electricity, and you at once possess greater mental power potential. When you subsequently trigger a secret mental power in you with the Miracle Mind Magic Stimulator, that secret mental power produces nerve-electricity dynamite in you and alters your physiological language into the right one to produce the right milieu in your brain for explosive mind magic.

How to Release the Secret Mental Powers
Strangled Within You by a Squeezing Spine

To release the secret mental powers strangled within you by a squeezing spine, you have to straighten your spine as much as possible back to a normal curvature. If your spine is pathologically displaced you need professional help, of course.

How a Secret Mental Power Can Heal Different
Ailments Through Their Different
Physiological Languages

When you are sick, in any way whatever, either your sympathetic or your parasympathetic nervous system prevails in that particular ailment. When you convalesce, the opposite system prevails and brings you back to health. When you get worse, the prevailing nervous system of that disease prevails in you still more. When the disease is chronic, both of these nervous systems are stable, but the one associated with the symptoms of that disease is the more "active" of the two. Most symptoms are departures from normal function.

The medical physician usually prescribes drugs *not* to cure a disease directly, but to normalize its symptoms. The body itself is then left unhindered to regain its normal functions, and thus to overcome the ailment. The chiropractor aims to do likewise through spinal adjustment. The psychiatrist may use hypnotism, suggestion, or other psychotherapy (sometimes even by prescribing drugs), to help the mind reduce the symptoms of the "disease" and let the tissues normalize themselves. In each isntance, the main goal is to normalize the symptoms—or to alter the negative physiological language of the malady into a positive one, so that it may speak the language of health. Once this goal is achieved, the diseased tissues flash this healthy alteration, through your nerves of pain and temperature, etc., to your conscious mind. As a result, you *feel* different when your raging fever diminishes, or when your heart beats more quietly, or when your convulsing stomach relaxes. Your conscious mind then automatically acquires *the necessary secret mental power*, or *the confidence in your body*, to overcome that disease. It flashes this conviction to your *sub*conscious mind. Your subconscious mind then relays it to whichever nervous system in you prevails in that particular disease, and normalizes it. That alters your negative physiological language into a positive (or healthy) one. Your body then proceeds to heal itself.

How to Induce the Nerve Fibers of any Secret Mental Power to "Line Up Right" in Your Brain and Bring About the Miracle of Mind Magic

Whenever you think, a certain number of the thirteen billion nerve fibers in your brain line up in one particular pattern out of a possible million others, to code your thoughts. They may fail to do so, however, for numerous reasons, the most important of which is "competing ideas." Your brain, for one thing, contains more than 10,000,000 nerve cells. A computer contains a few hundred thousand parts (which are equivalent to nerve cells). For some time, then, your brain will remain at least 10,000 times more complex than a computer. That is why you cannot always solve your problems readily, and why you frequently resort to the "incubation effect"—or you leave a problem you can't solve and let the answer pop into your mind several hours, days, or weeks later. During that period of time, something which inhibits the solution of your problem loses its strength and enables the solution to take place automatically in you (such as, through your subconscious mind). Therefore, the solution to the problem *was in your mind all the time*, but for some reason, it was inhibited by competing ideas.

It stands to reason, then, that a secret mental power strong enough to *remove* that inhibition would let your *conscious mind* solve your problem *right then and there,* without your having to wait for hours, days, or weeks! That speedy solution can be brought about by the Miracle Mind Magic Stimulator. With that "magic instrument" you can induce the nerve fibers of *any* secret mental power to "line up right" inside your brain and trigger the mind magic of your *conscious mind* into action *instantly.*

The Three Steps of the Miracle Mind Magic Stimulator to Trigger Your Secret Mental Powers

You will create the Miracle Mind Magic Stimulator with three important steps. The three steps are very simple and very much alike; but you will be taught how to intensify them, with a little practice, so they can alter your body functions rapidly into the right physiological language necessary for whatever secret mental power you wish to trigger into action. Practice them alone in your room, so that you can soon apply them readily in public.

Here, first, are the three easy, but fantastic, steps of the Miracle Mind Magic Stimulator. Just read them through to begin with, but then apply the steps in a regular, conscientious manner.

Step 1:
  (a) Think of whatever goal, dream, or wish you want to come true, for about five seconds.
  (b) Immediately visualize it as coming true, and maintain that vision for about four seconds.

Step 2:
  (a) Think of that goal, dream, or wish *again* for about five seconds. But this time dig deep into your conscious mind for it and drag out its details.
  (b) Immediately visualize it *again* as coming true, and maintain that vision for about four seconds. But, visualize it *far more clearly and completely* than before. Let the details fit into it, as if it were actually occurring.

Step 3:

    (a) Once more think of that goal, dream, or wish, for about five seconds. But this time dig so deeply into your mind for it that you extract *every possible detail* about it.

    (b) Immediately visualize it once more as coming true, and maintain that vision for about four seconds. But, visualize it so thoroughly in every detail that it seems to "come true" right before your eyes.

Those, simply explained, are the three steps of the Miracle Mind Magic Stimulator to trigger your secret mental powers.

How to Practice Intensifying the Miracle Mind Magic Stimulator

Practice the Miracle Mind Magic Stimulator with one goal, dream, or wish of yours after another to guide you in one step after the other. Practice each step until you perform it easily, quickly, and with a visual intensity that practically "lifts" your head off your body. If at first you can't execute each step in he number of seconds stated and do it thoroughly, take more time. Spend up to a half minute with each whole step at first, if need be. But reduce that time soon because your mind will fatigue, otherwise, and be bored from dwelling so long on something so abstract as a mere vision. Your goal, dream or wish will flow lazily through your mind when you commence the practice, but probe into it and see every side of it. Only then will your vision of it bring out every facet of the secret mental power which your Miracle Mind Magic Stimulator will trigger into action, to make it come true.

If your goal, dream or wish is a big promotion in your job, for instance, visualize it, in the first step, as coming true, with your receiving the big promotion.

In the second step, visualize yourself doing successfully (but in swift sequence) whatever you *must* do to secure that big promotion.

In the third step, visualize yourself *doing successfully* what you *must* do to secure that big promotion. Do it swiftly, but so realistically that your whole body feels as if you have *actually earned* that big promotion already through your efforts and *cannot help but receive it now*!

Do it whether your goal, dream, or wish is to make a big sum of money and retire, or is to win the person you adore, to draw an influential backer behind you, to control others swiftly, to control nervous tension and worry, to use the most sensible judgment in anything you undertake, to act most wisely in any future plan you have, to rout nagging pain and minor illness, for sexual vitality and marital bliss, to master a new skill expertly, to keep eternally "young."

Practice visualizing each of the three steps with the ever-increasing conviction, from step to step, that each one is, will, and has come true. Then the vision of its becoming a reality will stand out so clearly before your mental eyes that your whole body will respond to it by feeling as if the goal, dream, or wish has *actually occurred*!

When you narrow down the visualizing time to the five and four second sequences, your conscious mind will dwell on each step long enough to saturate your subconscious mind with it. Your physiological language will then respond in full and create the right millieu for the secret mental power you have triggered.

The Secret of the Power of the Miracle Mind Magic Stimulator

The secret of the power of the Miracle Mind Magic Stimulator lies in the principle of physiological power magnification, which has already been established scientifically with one organ of the body after another. For example, if *two* sensory nerves connect with *one* motor nerve (which supplies a muscle), the muscle will *not* contract when *either one* of the sensory nerves is stimulated alone. But it contracts when *both* of them are stimulated simultaneously. This phenomenon is called "summation." It amounts to a physiological power magnification. All nerves, too, require a certain amount of stimulation before they will transmit a command to an organ or a muscle. This is known as "the threshhold stimulus." Weaker stimulations will be *ignored* by the nerves. Your sympathetic nervous system will *not* activate your body to fight or flee if the alarm it receives from your body or your mind is too weak for it to respond to it. The alarm which your sympathetic nervous system receives has to be strong enough to magnify its physiological power before it will accelerate your heartbeat, to pump more blood into your muscles to meet the emergency, to constrict the capillaries in your skin and viscera to make more blood available to your muscles, or to speed up your liver's metabolism of blood sugar to supply your muscles with more energy to fight with, and so forth.

How the Miracle Mind Magic Stimulator Works

With the Miracle Mind Magic Stimulator, you bring about the necessary physiological power magnification which your body needs to alter its physiological language, and create the proper milieu in which to trigger the right secret mental power you need for your goal, dream, or wish. Your normal self alone will not flash into your body a strong enough stimulation to cause it to alter its physiological language sufficiently for that. Your acquired lack of confidence in your innate ability or in your prospects to achieve your aims restrains your mind from flashing such a powerful stimulation into you. With the Miracle Mind Magic Stimulator, however, the vividness of the vision of success which you create for your goal, dream, or wish is so *savagely real* that your whole body responds to it as if that vision has already come true, and actually *changes* you into the person you would then become. As a result, you automatically acquire that person's physiological language!

That's why you *must create* the Miracle Mind Magic Stimulator in three steps. Each step multiplies the seeming reality of the previous one, until your final vision in Step 3 seems so real to you that it *compels* your body to alter its physiological language, *despite itself*. That immediately converts you into the very person who *can* achieve your goal, dream, or wish.

Importance of Your Mastering the Three Steps Now

Master the three steps of the Miracle Mind Magic Stimulator now. You will use them repeatedly to trigger your different secret mental powers. In each consequent lesson you will be taught, first, the different methods (scientifically refined) which different people have used to attain amazing successes in their goals, dreams, or wishes. Then you will be shown *how to trigger* the right secret mental power for each with the Miracle Mind Magic Stimulator. You will soon *be* the very person you have *always hoped to be*!

Lesson 4

How to Use Your Mental Power of Intellectual Leverage

Without intellectual leverage you are like a person controlled by instinct, without a reasoning mind. You move, act, eat, live, and love like a lower form of life; you learn comparatively little from life and remain on the same level intellectually all through it. You are no better than the average students when the teacher instructed them as average students instead of as geniuses. When the teacher instructed them as geniuses, however, their stimulated minds transformed them into geniuses. Their hidden powers were awakened! They now possessed intellectual leverage! They were now deeply thinking beings, hungering for more knowledge!

Intellectual laziness is boring and wearisome. When you stop thinking keenly you either yawn or feel like "going out and raising the devil." Others resort to drugs, perversions, kleptomania (stealing), and sadistic crimes "just for the heck of it."

You can't suppress and forget your hidden powers. They will explode out of you in some way, and possibly wreck you. But when you release them with intellectual leverage, they change your whole life into a delightful adventure of discovery, of startling understanding of other people and world affairs, and of easy, magical achievement of your every goal, dream, or wish!

Without even trying to, you will find yourself outsmarting people in every kind of competition, seeing through the veils of deception in different matters, protecting yourself against different influences, and being admired and listened to by everybody.

You promptly acquire the confidence of being able to take care of yourself and hold your own in any situation. You are completely changed from an instinctive, blindly-acting earthworm into a veritable wizard to whom nothing is impossible. The secret mental power of intellectual leverage is truly the greatest miracle-mind creating power ever bestowed upon the human mind!

The Amazing Profits from Using Intellectual Leverage

The profits of every kind which certain people have gained from intellectual leverage are truly fantastic. With it they "righted" their relationships with others and acquired their admiration and respect. They took the right directions to big success, got rich fast, and retired early. They defended themselves against physical attack and swiftly "disarmed" their foes. They controlled their unhappy moods and became calm and contented. They recovered from business or health disasters and climbed to greater heights than ever before. They studied their perplexing problems and solved them to their greatest gain. With intellectual leverage, you can stop being upset or misled by anything, for you will "see the unseen" in it and turn it to your advantage. Intellectual leverage is truly a miracle of mind magic and this book shows you how to make use of it in your daily life.

The Great Opportunities Missed from Lack of Intellectual Leverage

From the dawn of time, intellectual leverage has been the decisive tool in the lives and fortunes of men and women. Had Adam applied it to Eve, he would not have bitten the apple. Had Eve applied it, she would not have listened to Satan. Had Othello applied it, he would not have fallen victim to the wiles of his best friend, Iago. Caesar and Brutus, Macbeth and Lady Macbeth, and many others would have escaped their tragic fates had they applied it to their close friends and associates. Millions of broken homes could have been saved by the parties using intellectual leverage. Swindlers, embezzlers, and confidence men make illegal fortunes by hoodwinking victims who fail to examine them with intellectual leverage. Other people let their opportunities of making fortunes slip by—their chances of creating lucrative inventions dissipate—because they don't apply intellectual leverage. You and everybody else have, at some time in your lives, the chance to get staggeringly rich or to establish a connection that could change your whole future for the better. You miss it because you lack the intellectual leverage to analyze the opportunity with the eyes of a seer. Similar opportunities are continually around you, but without intellectual leverage to take advantage of them, or even to recognize them before they pass by, you remain comparatively poor, mediocre, and discontented.

What Intellectual Leverage Is

Intellectual leverage is the secret mental power to weigh every problem in your life with such cold objectivity that you overlook no side of it. It forces you to shed all sensitivity to the cold, hard truth about anything. It prevents you from favoring the side of an issue which primarily flatters your ego, and from scorning the side that does not. It is of inestimable value to you because, by facing the naked truth about anything, you can more accurately predict its possible future and act on it to your utmost advantage. While other people react to that person or event emotionally, with little or no objective reasoning, with intellectual leverage *you* rid yourself of all emotion in regard to him (or it) and accept the disheartening truth in regards to him (or it), and turn threatened impending disaster into timely profit. Intellectual leverage easily disciplines you into the habit of sheer, cold logic, without the pain of panicky thinking.

Why You Lack Intellectual Leverage

To develop the secret mental power of intellectual leverage with psychology, philosophy, or sheer logic, however, is a grueling experience. Like everybody else, you are plagued with your own passionate likes and dislikes. In politics, you favor a certain party and certain principles. You do likewise with everything that touches your everyday life. Some of these emotional reactions may be natural to you. You might be a brunette, for instance, and be naturally attracted to blondes. You might own real estate and vote for the party that promises to lower the property tax. You might have been raised in a particular religion and subconsciously disapprove of the others. You might have been cheated in the past by someone from a particular group, race, or nationality, and now distrust all those belonging to it. You might have lost money investing in the past, and now you dread investing in anything. You might have vacationed somewhere when the weather was terrible, or met some obnoxious visitors there, and detest the locale forevermore.

Similar unfortunate experiences stunt your natural secret mental power of intellectual leverage, and leave you with crippled thinking. With intellectual leverage, in contrast, you would examine closely everything that affects you—*even that which you think you already understand.* Only then can you analyze effectively the important movements of your day and profit from them without limit. You will then lift yourself above the "herd mind" and anticipate the fantastic changes taking place anywhere, and reap the harvest of your insight and foresight. Even if you know little about the question at hand, with your resulting fearless, factual logic, you will detect the inconsistencies of the so-called experts.

How to Acquire Intellectual Leverage

Here is the easy way to develop the secret mental power of intellectual leverage.

- Stop forming spontaneous conclusions about anything.
- Investigate *unemotionally* the other side of it first.
- If it concerns someone else, put yourself in *his* (or *her*) place.
- Pretend to be him (or her). View yourself as living as he does, holding his job, married to his (or her) mate, and having his children and philosophy. Forget that you are you. In your own mind, even refer to yourself by his name.
- Then saturate yourself with the problem and see it through *his* eyes.
- Record what *he* thinks about it, or about you.

— You are then prepared to handle him to advantage in every move he makes.

Don't rashly discredit every opinion you may already hold about the question or problem, but subject it to close scrutiny. Like almost everybody else, your opinions are based considerably upon your own unique experiences. That's why they may be somewhat unscientific and unintentionally prejudicial. To base your future actions on them is to invite failure in business and in social life, and to handicap your best talents and fail to gain from your best opportunities. Most "scientific" conclusions are seldom continued to be accepted with the passing years. Every five years, most new books outdate the old. They disprove a good part of the old findings and reveal new conclusions. When studying the inexact sciences, in particular, remember that a good part of the material may not be true. But since you can't wait five years to find out which part of it is not, let intellectual leverage guide you in what part of it to accept. You can then anticipate many changes which may occur in that knowledge, and act profitably thereby. The investor who anticipated the invention and development of television years ago disposed of his radio, motion picture, and book publishing stocks at their zenith. With intellectual leverage again, years later, that same investor could have anticipated the decline of television, the rise of song recording stocks and of paperback book publishing.

How to Apply Intellectual Leverage on People

Practice accepting even the opinions of qualified experts as inconclusive. Much of their advice is based on the texts they studied in school and is colored with a certain amount of outdated knowledge. If you have time, read up a little on your problem before calling on a professional man for his services. Even though a little knowledge is a dangerous thing, you will then weigh better the help he gives you.

But don't degenerate into a doubter or a cynic and pick senseless arguments with others. On the other hand, close your mind to nothing until you weigh both sides of it. If people prove hard-headed or stubborn, confine your investigation to books and other authentic sources. The librarian will help you in the library.

It is impossible of course, always to select the best authorities, for the ones who are revered today may be condemned five years from now; but you will still see several sides of the question. Everybody makes mistakes, but he who makes the less serious ones wins.

Fundamental Rule

The rule to follow is: make an independent investigation of everything, if possible, before seeking advice on it. Don't dodge the naked facts, no matter how they hurt your feelings or run counter to general opinion. Accept the brutal facts as you find them and act with your own eyes wide open. *Then* you will act to your best advantage.

You will still make mistakes, naturally, for your intellectual leverage won't be 100 percent logical. But your conclusions will increase in accuracy, while those of the prejudiced and opinionated will not. *You* will, therefore, make less serious mistakes than they; you will take more decisive steps ahead, and achieve your goals, dreams, or wishes faster and easier than they. *You* will be guided by level-headed decisions, while *they* will be *misguided* by their childish stubbornness or pessimism. *You* will adjust yourself readily to any eventuality, while *they* will be panic-stricken by it. *You* will rise from the smoldering ruins of your life to greater heights than ever, while *they* will be driven to drink, vice, or suicide. *You* will perceive the *reasons* for your disastrous mistakes swiftly after they occur, while *they* will stay blind to their own mistakes and blame other people, the government, or fate. *They* will learn nothing from their failures, while *you* will capitalize on them by coming back and using them to full advantage *by avoiding making those same mistakes again*!

How to Amass Wealth with Intellectual Leverage

Intellectual leverage keeps you walking the line of intellectual sanity. Don't sink below it in helpless rage and despair, and don't leap above it with dreams impossible of realization. Don't stifle your goals, though, and accept a dull, average life. As stated before, everyone has a chance to make a handsome fortune. (A fortune may be considered to be anything from $50,000 up.) He misses it because he is too cautious to act, or lacks enough confidence in himself, or ignores the opportunity for another one which he erroneously believes is better, or lacks the initiative to strike out on something new.

Lack of capital is not always to blame. Great enterprises have been started on $200 or less, providing you use your own labor—and sometimes even your family's part-time labor. Enterprises which are started on huge capital may waste considerable funds in reckless experiment, and frequently collapse. The one that lasts is guided by intellectual leverage. Without surplus capital, you will use intellectual leverage (or your logical thinking based upon the concrete facts you gather from limited but fearless experiment) to help you succeed in your plans, with the least waste of time, effort, and expenditure. You then discover more swiftly the effective methods to proceed with them. You might squander your backing otherwise, and have to use intellectual leverage in the end to save yourself from ruin.

The more you know about anything (providing that your knowledge is as free as possible of emotion), the better you can apply intellectual leverage to it and succeed sooner with it. If your knowledge of it is clouded with blind prejudice and outdated conclusions, however, it will handicap you when you use it by preventing you from applying your best talents to it. To acquire knowledge about anything too rapidly, therefore, is not always desirable. It is wiser to study it keenly and carefully, even if it takes you longer, and weigh every step you plan to use. Try to see in each step *beyond what others have seen*, and use what you see *before* others do.

How to Apply Intellectual Leverage for Self-Defense

As startling as it might seem, intellectual leverage is as effective for self-defense as physical resistance. Physical resistance, in fact, is of little value without intellectual leverage. When surprised by a bully, you tend to become emotional and lose self-control. If you try to protect yourself physically with that frame of mind, you will forget everything you learned about self-defense.

Your aggressor, though, can be whittled down with intellectual leverage, even without striking a blow. When he approaches you, don't grow terrified, even if he is twice your size. Just stand still and take a subtle, deep breath to quiet your racing heart. Stare at the hoodlum as if at a lamppost, and see him as just another living body with a brain and a nervous system which rushes commands to his muscles to harm you. That same brain, though, can rush commands to his muscles *to leave you alone.* Right now, besides, it is tightly keyed-up and easy to influence. If you offer him physical resistance, his brain will respond instinctively with violence. If you cower, on the other hand, it might command his muscles to lambast you with sadistic joy. If it finds you cool as a cucumber, however, it will stop toning up his muscles with the confidence to act.

That momentary hesitation on his part is all you need to gain control over his highly keyed-up brain. Keep staring at him, *relaxed and breathing normally.* To achieve that, breathe slower than normal to keep enough air in your lungs. That keeps your physiological language normal enough to keep your brain cool and your eyes staring steadily at him. Your accoster's keyed-up brain will be flooded with doubts and will pour commands of hesitation into his muscles. Continue staring unflinchingly at him, meanwhile, and his subconscious mind will soften like that of the subject under hypnosis, and his muscles will lose their abnormal muscle tone, and his body will lose its explosive urge to attack you. You can ask him quietly now, "Want a light?" He will take advantage of the opportunity to apologize and "light out," fast.

How to Apply Intellectual Leverage to Control Your Unhappy Moods

When you are unhappy your brain secretes many different chemical substances, or a different variety of them. These fill it with waste products and cause tension in it. If continued for hours, your head (particularly your forehead area) will ache, because it is deprived of its normal oxygen supply. That adds pain and discomfort, and worsens your unhappy mood.

Intellectual leverage is the perfect weapon against that calamity, because it fills your mind with the *opposite* inclination of that worry or bad mood. If you are reflecting about something depressing, for instance, with intellectual leverage you can reflect about something that brought you overwhelming joy *and hold on to the thought*! Your depressing thought will, as a consequence, lose its grip on you, and fresh blood will pour into your brain and wash out its stagnant waste products quickly. Your unhappy mood will vanish with them.

How to Trigger the Secret Mental Power of Intellectual Leverage with the Miracle Mind Magic Stimulator

When you need intellectual leverage most, you will find it hardest to trigger. When you are being savagely stubborn, blind with anger, welled-up with prejudice, or your thinking nullified by fear, your financial acuity annihilated by the personality of the opposition you face, it is difficult to apply intellectual leverage. Your ego would be shattered then if you agreed with yourself that you were wrong; your temper would be impossible to harness; your dreads would be out of bounds. On such occasions your body speaks a fight-or-flight physiological language, in which your sanity is all but paralyzed, your heart pounds furiously, your breathing is fast and shallow, your muscles overtaut, and you feel as if ready to burst.

Procedure to Follow for Intellectual Leverage

To overcome such a negative physiological language at once, imagine the goal, dream, or wish you desire. Hold it for five seconds. Then visualize yourself changing into the person who *can* achieve that goal, and maintain that vision for four seconds. Repeat that procedure three times, as you did when you practiced the Miracle Mind Magic Stimulator. Intensify it each time, so that you actually *see* your goal coming true right before your eyes! If you are confronting the person, as in self-defense, visualize that change so clearly the *first* time you envision it that you actually perceive the bully relax and his threats dissipate. That would be long enough for him to hesitate in his aggression and would be long enough for you to control him. Practice with other situations in which intellectual leverage can save the day for you and bring you stupendous gains.

Below are case histories of people who used the secret mental power of intellectual leverage profitably for typical situations. Their names have been changed for obvious reasons.

How Businessman Donald Z. Came Back from Disaster to Make Far More Money, Easier Than Ever

Donald Z. had a business of his own, but made wrong decisions at critical times, allowing himself to be guided more by wishful thinking than by cold logic. He faced ruin and was already in his fifties.

I taught Donald the secret mental power of intellectual leverage and told him to review his plight with it. With intellectual leverage, he discovered that his knowledge of his business was colored by prejudice and outdated conclusions. Led chiefly by greed, he had not carefully weighed his plans for it. With intellectual leverage, he reconsidered them and tried to see in them *beyond* what others had seen. To apply it easier he triggered it with the Miracle Mind Magic Stimulator and altered his negative physiological language into a new, positive one.

Before long, one striking idea after another seized him. Within a few months Donald was making far more money—and *much easier*—than he ever had. "And I've hardly put half my new plans into action yet!" he said excitedly.

How Peter N. Balanced His Emotional Thinking and Pleased His Customers

Peter N. was in a service industry. He had quit his job and invested all his savings in this new venture, for he was determined to be his own boss. "How else can one get rich?" he exclaimed.

But his rivals were taking the business away from him. He couldn't lower his prices any more and still clear a profit. His customers, too, were "penny pinchers." He sighed in despair; disaster stared him in the face.

His unhappy mood, I told him bluntly, chased his customers away. "But how can I seem happy?" he cried. "I'm going bankrupt fast!"

I taught him the secret mental power of intellectual leverage. With it he put himself in his customers' places and promptly understood what they expected of him. Reluctantly, he changed himself to present *that* picture of himself to them. I told him to forget his competitors, because worrying about them only ruined his positive physiological language. He triggered this change within instantly when customers came in. It not only saved his business, but soon brought him more business than any of his rivals.

How John B. Tamed His Attacker in a Flash

John B. was hurrying home one night after working overtime. He was rejoicing over the extra pay, for it was costing him quite a sum to send his three children to college. A big, thick-shouldered man with a shaggy, long-hair look stopped him the moment he stepped out of his car. John saw himself being robbed, and beaten up as well.

But he had worked his program for intellectual leverage well for his job advancement. So, he stood quietly and took a deep, subtle breath to still his frightened and racing heart. He stared at his accoster, meanwhile, as if he were just another human being with a brain (even if a poor one) and a nervous system which rushed its commands to his muscles—in this case, to do violence to John. But that same brain, John reminded himself, could rush commands to those same muscles *to leave John alone!* That recollection kept him cool—and confused the bully.

That momentary hesitation was all John needed. Calmly, he said to the man, "Want a light?"

The hoodlum seemed utterly bewildered, sputtered some apologies, and left in a hurry.

SUMMARY OF THIS SECRET MENTAL POWER

Intellectual leverage is a supreme secret mental power for you to amass wealth, for your self-defense, and to control your unhappy moods. To acquire it most easily, follow these simple routines:

1. Confront the frightening problem that stands in your way, fearlessly and unemotionally.
2. Cast off all blind prejudice against it, no matter how it pains your ego.
3. With the Miracle Mind Magic Stimulator cast out the fight-and-flight reaction in you to the problem and replace it with the right, positive, healthy physiological language.
4. You will see the problem in an entirely different light.
5. Solve it in that new light.
6. You will turn that problem to your utmost advantage and make great gains.

Lesson 5

The Secret Mental Power to Overcome Your Confused Thinking

Confused thinking rips your hidden mental powers into shreds as brutally as if your brain had been scientifically chopped up and the pieces rearranged aimlessly around in your head. You may still move, talk, act, eat, live, and love, but you behave like an incoherent mass under control of a mixed-up "Tower of Babel." You become so out-of-step with yourself, with others, and with practically everything else, that you are as pitiful as a blind man in the middle of a bustling boulevard. The least word you hear, the most minor influence you receive—in fact, anything and everything that reaches your sense organs—throws you into a big scare. Every molehill grows into a mountain, and you don't know whether you are coming or going. Instead of facing life calmly and figuring things out with intellectual leverage, you arrive at one impulsive decision after another in problem after problem, and make so many mistakes that they practically leave you prostrated. Your hidden powers are of little value to you then and you wish you were dead. With the secret mental power to overcome and prevent confused thinking, however, you take firm hold of yourself and turn into a genius at anything you wish to, and realize with astonishing ease your every goal, dream, or wish. That's why this is a remarkable secret mental power to master.

People with seemingly no chance of getting anywhere, socially or in business, suddenly reached the heights "reserved"

63

only for the most lucky or the most gifted—when they simply overcame their confused thinking. Aspiring opera singers who had practiced desperately for years and failed to get anywhere suddenly understood how to "place" their voices and leaped past their musical rivals. Men who strove for years to invest profitably and failed suddenly "saw the mystery" and turned into million-aires in a few years. Businessmen who had failed again and again suddenly realized how to feel the public pulse and made fortunes. Sheer amateurs in a hobby, like golf or stock-market trading, suddenly "went professional" and made good, or traded with startling gains. Frustrated salesmen suddenly zoomed to earning over $50,000 a year. Men and women who were shunned by the opposite sex were suddenly living the social lives they always wished to lead. In practically everything in life there are people who were failures for a long time, and suddenly were incredibly successful by overcoming and preventing confused thinking. It will pay you in cold, hard cash—and in other big ways—to master this secret mental power *perfectly*, as unfolded in this book.

How Confused Thinking Usually Starts

You cannot develop the mind of a genius in anything successfully with confused thinking. The vast majority of people accept the declarations of one admired authority, then turn around and accept the conflicting ones of another. Their minds are muddled by contradictions. They hardly reason, and they form emotional conclusions about practically everything. Some do well in some unimportant phases of their own fields, but are "far off" in other "payoff" phases of it. So they fail to rise as high as they could. They become fanatical in their confusion, and are swayed by braggarts or demagogues. Their originality is stifled, their goals in life unreachable, and they are utterly confused.

Why You May Be Confused

You are also somewhat guilty of confused thinking because you, too, have acquired much of your knowledge about life and people under *emotional circumstances*. It might have started from your faulty or misguided understanding of certain controlling facts in your life, or from improper rearing or home conditions, or from shocking or discouraging "blind-end" experiences. When you are young, you assign overimportance to many a trifling situation, and it affects your behavior for the rest of your life. Erroneous advice from pessimists, too, may convert you into a defeatist. Wrong counselling from heavily opinionated people is equally to blame. Immoral or "sophisticated" companions may initiate you into an entirely different person and alter your whole physiological language, especially whenever you take any important action. It clouds your mind, while the mind of a genius has to be crystal clear in achieving a goal.

How to Overcome Confused Thinking

To rid yourself of confused thinking, follow the simple program below:

Step 1: *How to fill yourself with interest in a "repugnant" subject.* List, on paper, one thing after another that angers or frightens you. As an aid, scan through the daily newspaper. Pause at any article that does not interest you and compel yourself to read it. If you are a man, you will probably want to skip past an article about women's styles. To you it tediously fusses with different fabrics, garments, threads, needles, and other unmanly stuff, despite the tendency towards the "unisex." Read the article, nonetheless, and try to basically understand it. (If you are a woman, you might read an article about football or boxing.)

Various Phases of Interesting Topics

Women's fashions, you will find, are not concerned wholly with fabrics, threads, and thimbles. (Neither is football or boxing concerned only with big, strong men.) Women's fashions are concerned also with psychology, physics, chemistry, geometry, trigonometry, art, economics, world affairs, philosophy, accounting, esthetics, religion, geography, meteorology (the science of the weather), war, history, creative design, predictions of the future, prevalent moods and tastes, furniture, architecture, inventions, advertising, and heaven knows what else. Indeed, there is hardly a subject it is not concerned with. A clothing manufacturer or a fashion designer needs a wide variety of knowledge. He also needs extraordinary watchfulness and originality (as does an athlete).

There is nothing strictly effeminate about women's fashions, either. (There is nothing downright bestial about playing football or boxing, either.) The clothing industry is one of the biggest in the world, *and it is owned by men, for the most part.* It is big because everybody in civilized society wears clothes, and because clothes wear out, change with the seasons and the weather, with the occasion, and with the wearer's age. (Football, boxing, baseball, and other "manly" sports are also popular all over the civilized world.) People, too, tire of the same styles; but since just so many styles are possible, the designer has to use the same ones repeatedly in different ways. (The football player and the boxer, too, can make just so many moves with his body and his limbs, and has to use the same ones repeatedly in different ways.)

Machinery, too, is used for making clothes—and machinery is a masculine interest. The inventor of the sewing machine reaped a harvest in money. Keen watching and unemotional judging enter into the scoring of a game or a prizefight. The fairest athletics judge can be swayed, despite himself, by many factors.

Hidden Defects of Confused Thinking

If you are a man, your confused thinking about women's fashions may have prevented you from commercializing on inventions for it which might have occurred to you right in your own home after looking at your wife, or on the street after observing other women. (If you are a woman, your confused thinking about the "brains" of athletically-inclined men may have caused you to underestimate the future prospects of a desirable suitor.)

Follow this procedure with everything you dislike. No matter how repugnant any material might appear to you, remember that *everything* is concerned with psychology, physics, chemistry, economics, art, and so on. You will then see it as *the other person* sees it, end your confused thinking about it, and break down the artificial wall it has erected between you. You might even find yourself suddenly growing enthusiastic about another career that might suit you better than the one you have.

Step 2: *How to fill yourself with interest in a "dry" subject.* Turn to another uninteresting article in the newspaper and compel yourself to read it and absorb it. (Read the banking reports if you dislike them.) You will also discover in it a wealth of information relating to world events, philosophy, geography, economics, and other subjects which do interest you. All "dry" subjects are vital to human life and world affairs. They are uninteresting to the one who is unfamiliar with them, because they are undramatized. When you approach them with a personal problem, however, you will find them gripping. Law throbs with human conflict, psychological and otherwise. Mystery stories are based upon their characters breaking laws.

Pharmacy is not a lifeless compilation of formulas for cures, but is intimately bound up with economics, psychology, civics, fashion, geography, warfare, meteorology, philosophy, and countless other subjects. *No subject*, in fact, is separate from all other subjects. *All* are interwoven with each other. Only in textbooks and for ready identification are they separated and divided up.

Life itself is a complex network of *everything* in the present happening *at once.* By viewing it as composed of absolutely separate and unrelated parts you become a victim of confused thinking, and fail to acquire the mind of a genius in anything you attempt. You then erroneously classify certain subjects as being either "manly" or "effeminate," interesting or dry, easy or difficult, when, in actuality, they all overlap one another. If some seem dry, blame their form of presentation and your own approach to them. When you approach baseball, for instance, you don't approach it through its history or through its physics. You approach it either through playing it yourself, through worshipping a current hero, through fanatically following the success of a local or favorite team, through watching or listening to the world series. Before long, you are up-to-date on baseball. But you understand little or nothing about the complex physics behind effective pitching or batting. You know little about the intricate economics of running the team. As a baseball fan, though, you would study these subjects with feverish interest if your main purpose was to find out how they affected the sport. Those subjects would no longer be dry to you. But if you studied them only *for their own sake*, you might find them dishearteningly dry.

The Secret of Interesting Yourself
in any Subject—Your Hidden Talent Opener

If you approached the whole law school curriculum just as you would to learn the law about some baseball rule, law would no longer be dry to you. You would be pursuing it from a *personal* point of view, not from that of dead abstractions, weighted down by conflicting statutes and differing judicial decisions.

Approach anything you tackle or study, then, from the *personal angle*, and you will find it *very interesting*. It will open fields of endeavor which have been closed to you and which have prevented you from developing your talents and your secret mental powers to the fullest.

While ridding yourself of confused thinking, though, don't insult other people. Don't try to straighten out your prejudices about different subjects by questioning people who may be as blind or as prejudiced against them as you. Go, instead, to the sources that favor that particular subject and read them. Don't ask other men about women's fashions, for example. Read about women's fashions yourself! Be your own judge of the new knowledge you acquire. Become an independent thinker! That is the first requisite for acquiring secret mental powers and the mind of a genius, and for profiting fantastically from the miracle of mind magic. Declare your intellectual independence from the rest of the world!

How to Resist Forming Confused Thinking
About any New Knowledge

Constantly resist the ruinous tendency to form confused thinking about new knowledge and to accept baseless opinions as infallible facts. Be eternally ready to distinguish between opinion and established fact. If undebatable proof is missing, suspend your final judgment on the assertion, no matter how eager you may want to believe it. Rise above what you are trying to believe, and see things as they are, not as you wish they were. Keep your eyes wide open and take advantage of the "unseen" opportunities which lie beneath the known facts. If your own friends insist on believing what they wish to believe, don't argue with them, but keep your suspended judgment to yourself. Don't let *your* secret mental powers, though, be chained down by confused thinking, and let *your* opportunities slip by, one after another. You can *still* pass the remainder of your life living off what you accomplish hereafter with the acquired mind of a genius.

How to Trigger Overcoming and Preventing Confused Thinking with the Miracle Mind Magic Stimulator

Whenever you are blinded by confused thinking, you become impotent and are tempted to do something rash and catastrophic. To avoid this peril, visualize the obstacle you face (like the dry subject or the perplexing difficulty) as if it is *something personal*—something that interests *you* intimately—and which you expect to solve easily. That is the goal, dream, or wish you seek. Hold this picture in your mind for five seconds.

Then visualize your mind becoming very cool and your body losing its impetuosity, so that you *become* the kind of person who can understand the dry subject or solve the perplexing difficulty easily. Maintain that vision for four seconds.

Repeat that procedure three times, as you did when you practiced the Miracle Mind Magic Stimulator, so that you actually *see yourself standing right before your eyes, changed completely into the kind of person who is not gripped by confused thinking.* Your heart will beat normally, your rashness and impatience will ease, and your body will speak the right physiological language. Shorten the time period of the practice until you can convert yourself into that kind of person in a few brief seconds. You will then reach the heights in anything "reserved" for the most lucky or most gifted.

Benefits of Overcoming Confused Thinking

Below are case histories of people who used the secret mental power to overcome and prevent confused thinking profitably for typical situations. The names have been changed for obvious reasons.

How Steve K. Made Seemingly Miraculous
Repairs and Grew Rich

Steve K. was an ordinary repairman in a much-needed service. He was conscientious and tried his best. He also knew his work. No single repair he saw, though, fitted the ideal classroom example. Each differed from the other, even if slightly, due to how the machine was used, by whom, and by the habits, personality, and emotional make-up of the machine's operator. "Emotional operators" subjected the appliance to sudden, impulsive jerks, which wore it down in one way. Placid operators wore it down in another way. To add to the complexity, some of the machines were used by more than one person, each of whom possessed his own individual habits and characteristics. Some people used them in cooler or dustier places than others. Other people used them too long before having them readjusted and overhauled.

And that was just tapping the endless differences that confronted the repairman with each repair job. No textbook could list them all, for there seemed to be as many differences between them as there were operators. The kinds of repairs needed were also constantly changing; new ones came up, while the old ones lessened because of better-trained operators and new improvements in the models. Steve was nearly in a frenzy every time he faced a new repair job.

I taught him the secret mental power to overcome and prevent confused thinking. When he triggered it with the Miracle Mind Magic Stimulator, his mind and body spoke a new physiological language. No longer did he become terrified when he faced a new job, but studied it *as if the machine belonged to him*, or to his wife, parent, or child, and as if he was bursting with eagerness to fix it right and enthrall them. He made seemingly miraculous repairs as a result. He was soon hounded by satisfied customers and had to raise his charges in hopes of enjoying some peace. In a few years he was rich.

How Gertrude Y. Found the Easy Way to Keep
Cool During any Crisis

Gertrude Y. had been married to Alex for thirty years. Then a much younger woman pursued him and threatened her home.

Gertrude realized that she had lost much of her youthful appeal over the years, and that an attractive young woman nearly half her age offered her keen competition. She was seized by one impulsive drive after another. She would kill that other woman. She would kill her Alex. She would kill herself. She would throw acid in that woman's face. She would take poison herself. She would leap out a high window.

She burst into hysteria alone on her bed and battered the pillow. She ought to go to a tavern and give herself to man after man. She was still attractive enough! She considered one wild solution after another, but none of them showed her how to hang on to her husband and her home.

When she called on me she refused to see a psychiatrist, she said, because she was not crazy! She had always been remarkably level-headed. But her present problem threatened everything she had lived for. She had dreamed of retiring with Alex within a few years and moving to a retirement paradise, doing a little travelling from there and coming back home now and then to see their children. But now she faced the prospect of drifting about aimlessly, like an abandoned old woman, her life plans gone with the wind!

Her Need for a Cool Solution Was Met
Through the Magic Stimulator

What she needed most of all, I replied to her, was a cool attitude to face her problem in the most logical and advantageous manner, and to overcome her confused thinking. Otherwise she would drive Alex away.

Gertrude agreed to practice the secret mental power and to see the problem from her *husband's* point of view. And then, to implant *that vision* into herself with the Miracle Mind Magic Stimulator.

She did so, and her maniacal physiological language altered into that of a cool person. Thereafter she glamorized herself tastefully to meet the competition and maintained a winning calm. Before long, Alex tired of the nagging demands of the other woman to leave Gertrude and marry her, and decided that he had married the right woman for him. He fell in love with Gertrude again. She phoned me excitedly to tell me that they were leaving on a second honeymoon to choose their retirement paradise.

SUMMARY OF THIS SECRET MENTAL POWER

To overcome and prevent confused thinking is the best way to tear yourself free from self-enslavement, unleash your hidden powers to the full, and blazon forth as the person you are naturally, but are afraid to act like. To acquire this secret mental power easily, follow these simple routines:

1. Look squarely at whatever is holding you back in anything and smothering you with feelings of inadequacy.
2. Decide whether your confused thinking is due to terror of a dry subject, or to an inability to reason effectively and prevent others from deceiving you, or to a tendency of yours to form confused thinking about any new knowledge.
3. Do the exercise in this lesson which rids you of that drawback, and be ready to make a comeback in your life, no matter how devastating a loss you might already have suffered in it.
4. With the Miracle Mind Magic Stimulator, normalize the negative physiological language that engulfs you whenever you fall victim to confused thinking.
5. With a clearly thinking mind, release your buried talents and *be* the person you *can* really be.

Go ahead and master this secret mental power.

Lesson 6

The Secret Mental Power of Psycho-Photographic Memory

Psycho-photographic memory removes the vague fog from your mind whenever you perceive anything, and registers a specific picture of it which carves itself indelibly in your conscious mind. You go through life, otherwise, seeing mechanically but not really seeing, dynamically, like a nearsighted person staring at an object outside his clear field of vision, or like a person without an extensive vocabulary who hears every word of a speech but knows the correct meaning of only a portion of them.

Your conscious and subconscious minds gather a wealth of impressions all during your life, but without psycho-photographic memory a big percentage of those impressions are *mis*impressions. You *will* see what you look at, all right, but you don't see all there is to see in depth, nor interpret accurately what you do see. Even if you stare squarely at what you see then, you see it no better than if your mind were distracted. Your lifetime experiences, as a result, are worth much less to you because what you conclude from them is not wholly accurate.

That's why some people profit remarkably from certain experiences, while others don't (and never do to their detriment). Some people, indeed, *lose* from certain experiences because they perceive them through vague mental fogs and, consequently, misinterpret them. They misconstrue the persons they see or think about, just as the lover sees his loved one always as beautiful, no matter how far from beautiful she may be. The doting mother sees her child as honest, no matter how dishonest it might be. There is no end of examples. With the secret mental power of psychophotographic memory you acquire *a new dimension of thinking* which bares to you a concealed world which you never before suspected. It brings you an unexpected power over people and over your social and business life which turns over a whole new leaf in *your* life. Practice and master this astounding secret mental power.

The Fantastic Profits from Developing a Psycho-Photographic Memory

With the secret mental power of psycho-photographic memory people who would have realized only mediocre dreams achieved goals far beyond their expectations. College heads with turbulent campuses brought them under control with seeming magic. Executives of tottering firms whipped up the support of their employees and weathered the worst. Professional men with wavering practices were "mobbed" with patients or clients. Small businesses, staggering under merciless competition, survived and built up big trades. Victims of robbery, assault, and other crimes against the person, when it was difficult to identify criminals, spotted them elsewhere later, even after these criminals were disguised. Ordinary-looking women enslaved much-pursued men. Mediocre artists, writers, or clothing designers made fortunes. Frustrated teachers gained the allegiance of most difficult students. Downtrodden subordinates were pushed up the establishment ladder by harsh superiors. Dissidents were drawn together to support controversial stands. Lonely older people were admired and sought after by exciting younger people. *In one thing after another, psycho-photographic memory spelled the difference between ignominious failure and success.*

The Nucleus of Psycho-Photographic Memory

A knowledge of lines and anatomical figures, and their emotional effects upon the observer, is of little significance to you unless you can store up a backlog of these in the endless combinations in which you encounter them in your everyday life.

Every human being consists of legs, head, arms, torso, features, and pigmentation; yet no two individuals look exactly alike. Many of them look alike to the untrained observer, to the stranger among alien people, or to those who have not studied enough art or anatomy; but to the detective, the artist, the writer, the teacher, the psychologist, the plastic surgeon, the fashion designer, the body builder, and others who have studied the outer aspects of different people, there is a perceptible difference in the appearances between even a pair of identical twins. These experts (academically-taught or self-taught in the secrets of this book) have trained their sights to detect minute differences in line movement and angle, and acquire indelible psychic memories for particular aspects of the different people they see or encounter. Even when they have not laid eyes upon a particular individual for quite some time, they recollect his outer aspect more accurately than the untrained person who saw him only yesterday.

The Failures of an Untrained
Photographic Memory

The untrained person's conception of someone he has seen alters markedly in the course of a few days. He even ascribes close similarities to individuals who look distinctly different from each other, except for possessing the same general complexion, height, or physical make-up. That renders very difficult the task of law enforcers to capture criminals. When a woman victim is asked to describe the fiend who assaulted and robbed her, she replies, for instance, that he was a "thin, red-haired man." When prodded for a more exact description, she grows desperate and demands that the police find him. She usually remembers his clothes well, but provides very little helpful detail about his skin, features (except the color of his eyes), voice, posture, or gait, which could single him out in a group of thin redheads. Her estimate of his height or weight is seldom trustworthy; she may call him "little" when he measures five foot eight or nine, or "stocky" when his face and neck alone are full. She may insist he weighs 200 pounds when he scales 165, or vice versa. Shocked by his action, she can hardly think straight anyway. Even at the line-up she is not too helpful. With the secret mental power of psycho-photographic memory, however, she would recall unusual features about him which could lead to his swift apprehension.

Even when women confront suspects at the line-up, they are not always sure of them and neither are men. Their recollections of them are too general to pinpoint the culprit. They end up accusing several different suspects and go to pieces trying to pick out the guilty one. If the accused can trump up plausible alibis, they have to be freed.

Such a typical response will handicap you (whether you are a man or a woman) in numberless life situations and rob you of many a significant social or financial opportunity. So practice and master this secret mental power, set out for you as follows.

How to Develop Your Psycho-Photographic Memory

Exercise 1. Sit down and relax, and stare at a picture on the wall. Now *turn away* and describe the picture to yourself. To gather an accurate record of your observation, jot it down on paper. Regularly force your mind to crystallize your thoughts into words. Use the dictionary or a book of synonyms and antonyms to help you. Nothing can develop your ability to think accurately better than to force yourself to express yourself on paper.

If the picture on the wall is the portrait of a person, mark down the color of his eyes, the shape of his nose, his hairline, the curve of his lips, the size, position, and prominence of his ears, the texture of his skin, his clothes, his expression, and the type of thoughts he was probably absorbed in at the time. Pretend that this man (if it is a man) has struck you down, robbed you, and fled. Identify him in detail now, so the police can positively identify him, even months later. Try to recall and jot down minute individual marks about him, such as a mole on his face, the shape of his nostrils, the slant of his eyes. Don't give up easily, but ransack your brain mercilessly about him.

Then *turn back* to the picture and check your description of him against it.

Exercise 2. Repeat Exercise 1, but use pictures of several different people. Perfect your "taking-in" ability, until you can absorb, at a glance, an astonishing amount of exact description of any person or object.

Exercise 3. Repeat Exercise 1, but do *not* write down what you saw, until the *next day.* Then see how exactly your mind remembers what you saw. Do this several times.

Now do it again and wait a week. Use a different picture every time. This exercise will compel your conscious mind to dig deeply into your subconscious mind to unearth what you observed in that brief flash.

Exercise 4. If you went somewhere today for the first time—even if just to a store or to some building—describe it as thoroughly as you can *on paper.* Writers, painters, and commercial artists do that regularly with places they have not seen for years.

Describe, similarly, places you visit regularly, such as where you work.

Check on these descriptions as soon as convenient, to test your psycho-photographic memory. Detectives check, in that manner, the stories of homicide suspects. They check the exact position of the furniture of the murder room and the suspect's estimate of the distances between the different pieces. The very fate of your life or of a dear one could rest upon similar evidence.

Exercise 5. Stare at a picture in a newspaper or magazine. Describe, preferably on paper, everything you observed in it. Compare your description with the picture. Find what you left out, or what you perceived incorrectly. (This will also train you against letting illusion or suggestion distort the keenness of your visual perception.)

Exercise 6. Repeat the previous exercise with other pictures, but allow yourself less and less time to stare at each.

Exercise 7. Try to estimate at a glance, from the picture of a crowd, the number of people in it. Then count them. Repeat this exercise with other pictures of crowds until you acquire astounding mass accuracy. You can have fun with your friends, too, by trying it with them and amazing them with your own "innate accuracy."

Magic Aids for Acquiring Psycho-Photographic Memory Much Faster

1. Increasing the width of a rectangle makes it appear lower than it is. Examples:

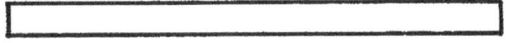

rectangle   *same rectangle with width increased*

Increasing its height, on the other hand, makes it appear narrower than it is. Examples:

rectangle   *same rectangle with height increased*

The above visual effects explain why broad-shouldered persons look shorter than they are, while narrow-shouldered persons look taller than they are.

The horizontal dimension is more resistant to this kind of suggestion than the vertical. It is easier for the narrow-shouldered man to look taller than he is, than for the broad-shouldered man to look shorter than he is.

2. A short man standing between two tall men

```
    **                              **
  ******                          ******
  * ** *              **          * ** *
  * ** *            ******        * ** *
  * ** *            * ** *        * ** *
    **              * ** *          **
    **                **            **
    **                **            **
```

looks shorter than he is. This is *contrast illusion*.

And, a tall man standing between two short men

```
                        **
                      ******
     **               * ** *                  **
   ******             * ** *                ******
   * ** *             * ** *                * ** *
   * ** *               **                  * ** *
     **                 **                    **
     **                 **                    **
```

looks taller than he is. This is known as *confluxion* or *assimilation.*

Other Magic Aids for Acquiring Psycho-Photographic Memory Much Faster

3. When a particular characteristic about a figure seizes your attention, your tendency is to single out this characteristic and overlook everything else about the figure. An example is that of the victimized woman calling her assailant-robber a thin, redheaded man, totally overlooking almost everything else about him.

The power of suggestion even increases this effect upon your sense perception. If you see a figure which is nearly round, you will probably perceive it as a perfect circle, or as a better circle than it actually is. If the figure is partly divided, you may perceive it as being completely divided. You tend to perceive the imperfect form as being more perfect than it is, and the nontypical form as being more typical than it is.

4. A more extreme obstacle to your psycho-photographic memory occurs when the figure you see suggests a different but more familiar object so clearly to you that you could swear you saw the second one instead. This occurred in the witch-hunts of past centuries, when people were accused of doing what their eavesdropping accusers *assumed* they did.

You cannot reason logically, create convincingly, or invent successfully, when you cannot perceive accurately. You will only cultivate ignorance then and be misguided in your efforts to accomplish what you would like to. So, train yourself to perceive everything you see with a keener eye and to detect the true structure behind every camouflage. Do so by mastering these magic aids.

The Serious Obstacles to Your Acquiring
Psycho-Photographic Memory

There are serious obstacles, though, to your acquiring this secret mental power. Some will be due to your miscalculation of the true size or mass of a person you see, and others to your personal refusal to accept what you see as fact. If you are a man and you see another man who is taller, broader shouldered, younger, and with more hair on his head than you, for instance, but who struts like a peacock, your possible jealousy of him, together with your inner resentment of his attitude, may blind you to his admirable physical attributes and you are not likely to perceive him as being as tall as he actually is, nor as broad-shouldered, and so on. If asked to identify him afterward, you are most likely to describe him to look the way you downgraded him in your mind. Such a picture of him becomes *your* permanent picture of him, even if you see him repeatedly afterward, because that's how you *wish* he looked.

On the other hand, your picture of the other person is distorted in *his* (or her) favor when you worship that person (such as someone you love, your favorite child, hero, or leader). You need psycho-photographic memory to "see" what you actually see and to prevent your emotional response from altering it. Trigger it with the Miracle Mind Magic Stimulator and stop holding yourself back socially, in business, in peace of mind, and in every other way possible.

How to Trigger Psycho-Photographic Memory
in You with the Miracle Mind Magic Stimulator

The serious obstacles to your acquiring the secret mental power of psycho-photographic memory fill you with the fury of your fight-or-flight sympathetics because they leave you bursting with anger, resentment, or envy; your muscles hypertense and your body speaks a wrong physiological language. The Miracle Mind Magic Stimulator counteracts them by filling you, in turn, with the kindness and sympathy of your easygoing parasympathetics. You become calm, your heartbeat and breathing normalize, your tense muscles relax, and your body speaks the right physiological language for this secret mental power and puts your conscious in the right mood for using it.

This is how to trigger psycho-photographic memory in you with the Miracle Mind Magic Stimulator. Your goal, dream, or wish, whenever you observe anyone or anything, is to appraise him (or it) with *unchallengeable fairness*! The easiest way to nullify any anger or resentment against, or any excessive effusion for, him (or it) that may arise in you is to *press two fingers of each hand hard against the corresponding thumb for three seconds.* That drains off the overemotionalism of your hostile sympathetics from you by exhausting it muscularly and leaves your mind unemotional toward him (or it). Then behold that person or thing with the magic aids for psycho-photographic memory and you will perceive him (or it) *objectively.* Maintain that vision for five seconds. Repeat that procedure three times, so that you perceive the person or thing with greater and greater objectivity. Your serious obstacles to acquiring psycho-photographic memory will vanish and you will instantly possess a secret mental power that can bring you gains far beyond your greatest expectations.

How Alice B. Spotted the Hoodlum Who Had
Attacked Her

Alice B. had gone Christmas shopping, and was weary from battling the crowds all day and hauling around the parcels she was bringing home. As she plodded with them from the bus, a man suddenly seized her purse. Alice screamed, and the thief struck her down. Next thing Alice knew, she was struggling on the icy sidewalk.

Later, two policemen helped her to her feet. She sobbed her story, and the policemen asked her to describe her assailant. But Alice could recall only that he was "a vicious hoodlum who should be locked up!" Under further prodding she cried that he was "blond and awfully strong!" She turned vindictive when questioned more specifically and demanded that the "brute" be caught. All told, he had stripped her of about $200, including the goods she had bought, and she was a plain, working woman!

After her bruises were treated, she came to me and wept out her story. I taught her the secret mental power of psycho-photographic memory. She mastered it quickly, returned to her quarters, sat down quietly, and relived her tragic experience. With the Miracle Mind Magic Stimulator she promptly normalized her seething physiological language and visualized her assailant no longer as a wild beast, but as a man who went out stealing and who also resorted to force. Her vengeful sympathetics lost their dominance over her and she calmly saw through the fog of bitterness that clouded her conscious mind. The savage picture she had concocted of the fiend vanished and she perceived now that his face had looked angelic and that his body had been slender and delicate-looking. But his motions had been swift and catlike. She phoned his new description to the authorities. A week later he was apprehended on a sidewalk several blocks away.

How Downtrodden Jim L. Was Pushed Up the
Corporate Ladder Fast by a Harsh Superior

Jim's plight grew worse by the day. His superior was driving him crazy with harsh criticism, with outrageous work demands and unnecessary inspections of his work. He even resented Jim's "coffee breaks" or his going to the fountain "so often" to take a drink. Jim prayed that the "old fogey" would retire, but he realized that that day was still many years away. Time and again Jim nearly "told him off," but how would he face his wife at home if he did? Neither did he relish the disheartening long tramping around the city searching for another job, as so many of his laid-off middle-aged contemporaries were doing. How, though, could he endure his impossible boss much longer? Any chance of further advancement for him in the firm for which he had worked so long, of course, was hopeless.

Jim explained his frustrating problem to me, and I taught him the secret mental power of psycho-photographic memory. He practiced and mastered it quickly. He then sat in his room and visualized his harsh superior as he perceived him every day—as the lean, wiry, sardonic dictator with curling, devilish lips and cruel, glinting eyes. Jim's hatred of him stimulated his fight-sympathetics; his heart and breathing speeded up, and his attacking muscles tensed tightly.

But Jim normalized this abnormal physiological language with the Miracle Mind Magic Stimulator by envisioning his superior treating him gently and considerately. That was his goal, dream, or wish. The bitter picture of his boss vanished and he perceived him now as a harassed superior deeply concerned about the future of the company. Instantly, no longer did the man appear lean and wiry, but as a rather well-porportioned man, with determined lips and the furrowed brows of a deep thinker. In fact, he was quite presentable.

At work the next day Jim ignored his superior's overbearing attitude and, at the right opportunity, subtly praised him for his appearance, accuracy, and mental keenness. The man's jaw dropped. His "bearing down" on Jim ceased soon after, and he started *helping* Jim instead of berating him. At the end of the month he recommended Jim for a raise at a time when others were suffering cuts in pay, and two months later pushed him into a much better position.

*How a Small Businesswoman Turned Threatened
Disaster into a Booming Success*

Thelma R. owned a small women's dress shop on a minor business street in a big city. Year after year she barely survived the competition of the giant downtown stores. This year, though, she faced a monumental decision which could either bring her a big harvest or put her out of business. A tremendous change in women's styles was planned for the clothing industry. The fashion designers were changing them from the recent extremely revealing cuts back to the conservative lines of before, as they had done repeatedly over the centuries. Thelma, like other retailers, had stocked up to a degree for the changeover, but her customers rebelled against it, calling the dresses "sleazy, dowdy, depressing."

The designers assured the frightened retailers, however, that the old-fashioned style would catch on again, that women had traditionally resisted style changes. When the present extreme style had been first introduced, they reminded the nervous retailers, it had met a ninety percent resistance! The "conservative style" was meeting the same amount now. But when women found no other style available, they would turn sheep again. "It's always this way at the outset!" the confident designers and manufacturers chanted. "Change is difficult to accept."

Thelma asked me what I thought. I urged her to learn and use the secret mental power of psycho-photographic memory to help her.

Thelma learned it fast, for she had to act in a hurry. With the Miracle Mind Magic Stimulator she normalized her frantic physiological language and perceived women's styles with the eyes of a *modern* woman buyer and wearer. She promptly detected the ecstatic sensual suggestions which the extreme modern style endowed the figure of the more boldly attention-seeking modern woman, and realized that the modern woman would rather die outright than be "buried alive" again in the comparatively modest rainments of yesteryear.

So Thelma ignored the designers and gambled everything on the modern clothes. The modern clothes won out. Thelma reaped such a big harvest that she was able to put a down payment to buy the fully-rented commercial building where her store had previously occupied little more than a cubbyhole.

SUMMARY OF THIS SECRET MENTAL POWER

With psycho-photographic memory you swiftly raise yourself out of the masses of people who are pinned down to mediocrity by their self-centeredness, and rise into the class who possess the golden touch with every move they make. To acquire this secret mental power easily, follow these simple routines:

1. Stare calmly at the person or thing that throws you into raring emotion or envy, or into blind effusion.
2. With the Miracle Mind Magic Stimulator trigger the right physiological language within you for perceiving him (or it) objectively.
3. Use the magic aids for acquiring psycho-photographic memory fast, and your conscious mind will perceive what you see with the well-balanced eyes of a King Solomon.
4. Affluence, popularity, and the long arm to capture violent criminals who victimize you, will all be yours, like true magic.

Secret Mental Powers for Profitable Concentration

Without profitable concentration you degenerate into a restless, flighty thinker who jumps from one thing to another, never fastening your thoughts long enough on anything to squeeze the full potential out of it. Everything soon bores you and you learn nothing you can rely on, for your thinking amounts only to a hurried scanning. You forget so much of what you study, observe, contemplate, or experience, that you waste your time on this earth. You engage in pointless escape dreaming, instead of on application which could reward you with a fortune-making invention, fad, or business, or an easy way to rise much faster in your career.

Without the secret mental power of profitable concentration, you gain no more than a lazy thinker who dodges vital issues and remains superficial and mixed up, and turns sour because "everybody" takes advantage of him. With it, though, you lift yourself out of the groaning majority, take the helm of leadership, and make a stunning profit in everything you undertake.

The Fantastic Profits from Using Profitable Concentration

The profits which different people made from the secret mental power of profitable concentration surpass belief. With it, people who could hardly understand the words in a book, much less define their meaning, glued their eyes to its pages, scanned through them, and passed the most detailed examinations on it. Others bored through dry, academic matter and discerned in it important fields for research as yet hardly tapped, and used them as springboards for remarkable new inventions, discoveries, or new avenues to stupendous profits. Others transformed otherwise boring material into lively episodes and went on to become highly-paid science-fiction writers. Or they extracted basic conclusions from them and became highly-paid designers, coaches of major teams, startlingly original architects, amazingly successful executives, financiers, generals, and the like.

Still others put this secret mental power to such sensational uses as solving baffling crimes or in tracking down and cornering well-concealed criminals. Still others used it to trap those guilty of the most ingenious swindles. They even used it to pursue criminals who had fled thousands of miles from the scenes of their deviltries without leaving a trace for the police to pursue. It is a secret mental power with which you can really perform "miracles." Let nothing stop you from mastering it fast.

How Unprofitably Your "Usual Self" Concentrates

You hardly suspect *how* unprofitably your average self concentrates most of the time. You do suspect that it does not concentrate as profitably as you would like it to, and you abhor anything that requires too much concentration from you. Textbooks, financial problems, investment decisions, practical plans for the future, social adjustments, schemes by others against you—these are but samples of the endless demands upon you for profitable concentration. They take the spice out of your life because they drag you away from a relaxed, pleasant mood and affix you into a taut, tense frame of mind.

The very verb "to retire" implies "to get away from it all,"—to get away from where you have to think strenuously to "make good" and "stay in the rat race." Your mind, as a consequence, builds up a revulsion against the very act of concentration, and your brain centers respond by commanding your body to revolt against it with a negative physiological language. Every time you are directed to learn something, or ordered to do this and not that, to say this but not the other, to act one way and not another, or to practice to excel at anything, you are compelled to stop being playful and relaxed and to discipline yourself in a mental strait jacket. And so you acquire a horror of concentration and don't concentrate profitably.

This horror grows over the years because your life grows more complex with time. You come to enjoy doing most what you have already mastered and that which you can do excellently with the least effort of concentration. But nothing remains constant. "Improvement" or "progress" never stops, and you can't ride on past knowledge for long before being left behind, outdated. Your number of brain cells, too, diminishes with the years, making concentration more laborious as you get older. That increases still more your horror of it. To concentrate profitably under those circumstances becomes more and more impossible, until you feel that you are too old and should "retire and let the younger crowd" take over.

All this happens to you because you did not master the secret mental power for profitable concentration. Actually, over the years, you should be able to concentrate *easier and easier*, for you are more experienced at it. But the wrong physiological language it has built up in you prevents you from enjoying it and profiting fantastically from it.

How to Use Your Secret Power to Concentrate Profitably

Within you is a secret power to concentrate *profitably*. With the right physiological language to stimulate it, you can be as different as night is from day, or as different as when you are asleep from when you are awake. When relaxed you are dominated by your parasympathetic nervous system. The pupils of your eyes are smaller (for you are less alert), your adrenal gland secretes less adrenalin (for you are in no fighting mood), your heart beats slower and less forcibly (and your coronary arteries are therefore narrowed), your bronchi are less open (for you breathe less rapidly), your stomach pours out more digestive acid (for you have a bigger appetite), and your whole digestive system is eager to digest and absorb your food. Blood is drained from your brain and muscles to flood and nourish your abdominal contents for that purpose. Your keenest power of concentration is simultaneously reduced, and your muscles lose muscle tone because you are not in a "fighting" mood. Your brain centers "fall asleep." Your body is speaking a lethargic physiological language.

But when you concentrate you are dominated by your *sympathetic* nervous system. Your pupils are larger (for you are keenly alert), your adrenal gland secretes more adrenalin (for you are in a fighting mood), your heart beats faster and more forcibly (and your coronary arteries are therefore dilated), your bronchi are wider open (for you breathe more rapidly), your stomach pours out less acid (for you have little or no appetite), and the blood vessels of your whole digestive apparatus narrow, as the blood is drained from them to your brain and muscles to nourish them during the expected efforts. Your body is speaking an excited physiological language.

You are automatically thrown into such a state when confronted with an emergency situation which you have to fight against or flee from. The power to concentrate like a "genius," then, is always present within you. You dislike arousing it beacuse it routs your feeling of relaxed laziness. But this feeling can spoil your chances of success when you are pursuing an important goal, dream, or wish, by letting your best opportunities for achieving it slip past you. Unusual opportunities of any kind don't come every day. They have to be "taken at the flood," as Shakespeare wrote. But, to take them at the flood, you have to know the secret rules for profitable concentration.

The Sixteen Secret Rules for Profitable Concentration

There are sixteen secret rules for profitable concentration which those who made fantastic profits from this secret mental power invariably applied. These rules will make your concentration scientific and put you on the swift road to realizing your goal, dream, or wish. When you trigger the right physiological language in you for profitable concentration with the Miracle Mind Magic Stimulator and apply the following rules, you, too, can gain fantastic profits. So study these rules carefully and use them in every situation you want to develop for your own benefit.

Rule 1: It is difficult to concentrate efficiently immediately after a hearty meal containing potatoes, onions, gravies thick with oil, or foods packed with fat. These foods digest slowly, on the whole, thereby depriving your brain of normal blood circulation for at least two hours.

Rule 2: Apples and other sleep-producing foods also dull the mind and make concentration more difficult until digested.

Rule 3: You concentrate best when you are thoroughly rested, such as after a good night's sleep, or after a short but pleasant nap.

Rule 4: You concentrate poorly when stunned by deep emotion or when worried about anything at all.

Rule 5: You concentrate poorly when plagued with chronic pain, such as from toothache, backache, or even from a throbbing corn or mild insect bite.

Rule 6: You concentrate best when strolling outdoors in a park or in the country, provided that you are safe and reasonably alone.

Rule 7: You concentrate excellently, too, on dark days, particularly when you are outdoors.

Rule 8: Quietude is an absolute must for best concentration.

Rule 9: Imbibe no spirited liquor or stimulants (including coffee, tea, or cocoa) before you concentrate. Keep your mind as clear, sensitive, and alert as possible.

Rule 10: Although smoking is detrimental to health, if you are a habitual smoker you might have (sad to say) to indulge in it when you concentrate, to "get your mind going."

Rule 11: Soft, classical music is conducive to concentration, while music with repetitious or noisy rhythm distracts the mind and routs concentration.

Rule 12: Certain colors help you concentrate better—*at first*. Once you are concentrating however, your mind forgets its surroundings if these don't change.

Rule 13: Lying on your back with your eyes covered from

light is conducive to concentration. If you are the type who falls asleep at the drop of a hat, though, you better take a walk or sit at your desk when you concentrate.

Rule 14: When concentrating or trying to, don't let your mind wander away and dote on your past, on imagined injuries, sexual vagaries, favorite sports, world tensions, or anything at all that takes your mind away from the subject of your concentration.

Rule 15: Narrow down your thinking to the very subject, or to the exact phase of the subject, on which you are concentrating.

Rule 16: To concentrate deeply, in brief, you have to resist fleeting attention and dulling interest. You have to bring your mind back, again and again, to the exact subject you are concentrating on, no matter how it bores you. When you grow bored with the subject, in fact, your mind will then suddenly come up with a new idea about it, because *then* your super-sensitized brain coding connects in the unique ways necessary to allow the new idea to flash across your conscious mind.

The Seven Secret Rules for Profitable Concentration for Research, Which Brought Great Riches to Different People

In order to extract the profitable orginality from any research, follow these secret rules, which have brought great riches to different people:

Rule 1: Don't read the research material from beginning to end, as if for pleasure, or as if to comprehend all of it. Just race through it instead, and pick out only the facts or principles that interest *you*, and concentrate on those alone.

Rule 2: Don't be satisfied with just one source of information, even if it agrees with yours. Examine all the sources you can find, and contrast them with each other.

Rule 3: Don't limit your investigation to modern authors or discoverers, either. Inspect the findings of authors on that subject for decades or centuries back. Most conclusions in anything, you will find, have been held and discarded repeatedly over the ages, so that the one held at present might have been condemned five years ago, or may be comdemned five years from now. That's why most textbooks are rewritten significantly every few years.

Rule 4: Don't be afraid to think independently and hold your own opinions or conclusions about any subject, even if it disagrees flagrantly with those of the "experts."

Rule 5: When you unearth the facts and material you seek, read them first to understand them. Then re-read them with a critical eye. Re-read them several times, if necessary, and re-examine them thoroughly. Strive to detect what the author left out, either through oversight or design, in order to prove his point. Unless you do that, you won't be able to evaluate his conclusions objectively.

Rule 6: Always jot down something about your findings, because the same thoughts never, or seldom, return to you later in exactly the same words. And the words in which they first come to you are usually by far the most explicit. Also, record the title of the source, its author, and page, so you can easily recheck the material later if you have to.

Rule 7: Whenever you take a brief respite during, or from, your labors of research, your mind will sizzle with creative ideas in it, with new conclusions, or with new reasons for *the* conclusions it already has arrived at. *Jot these down at once* before your mind cools off and your mental perceptions lose their keenness.

Follow these well-guarded rules and you will be brought riches in overflowing measure.

How to Trigger Yourself to Concentrate Profitably with the Miracle Mind Magic Stimulator

You need the power of concentration most when you are faced with a seemingly insurmountable obstacle, or when threatened with disaster if you don't achieve your goal, dream, or wish—or, at least, with a significant setback in life. You are therefore stricken with dread of failure or outright fear of catastrophe. Even if you were relaxed before, you are now gripped with fear.

Fear, like concentration, stimulates your sympathetic nervous system. But it is a *flight*, rather than a *fight*, reaction. Both reactions use your brains and muscles to their peak, for you use the flight one to run from the danger, and the fight one to combat it. But fear is a panicky stimulation, while concentration is a cool one. Both speak a similar physiological language in you; but once you go into action, with fear you dissipate your energy in one big hysterical effort, while with concentration you harness it and distribute it in productive action. Concentration is therefore a sympathetic nervous system reaction *under full control of the brain*! It puts your physiological language *under   the discipline of your brain*!

To put your physiological language *under the discipline of your brain*, trigger the secret mental power of profitable concentration in you with the Miracle Mind Magic Stimulator. *Then* apply the seven secret rules for profitable concentration for research and overcome the seemingly insurmountable obstacles of the threatened disaster.

This is how you trigger the secret mental power of profitable concentration with the Miracle Mind Magic Stimulator. Picture the goal, dream, or wish you want to achieve through concentrating. Hold that vision for five seconds. Now, visualize yourself *achieving* that goal with ease, and maintain the vision for four seconds. Repeat the procedure three times, as you learned from practicing the Miracle Mind Magic Stimulator. Intensify it each time, so that you actually *see yourself concentrating—and solving*—the petrifying problem before you. Your physiological language will alter quickly into the right one.

*How to Apply the Rules with Physiological
Language*

Now, apply *all* the secret rules of concentration just revealed to you with this new physiological language in you and attack the seemingly insurmountable obstacle or threatening disaster again. To your astonishment it will either solve itself easily now, or it will come so near to doing so that you need to repeat your vision of solving it *just once more* and it will solve itself for you, because you will have aligned in your brain the right codes for solving it! If you are tackling something very intricate, you might have to repeat the procedure several times—or even again several days later. But that would be unusual. Most of the time you will find the solution to your awesome problem as easily as described above.

Below are case histories of some of those who used the secret mental power for profitable concentration for typical everyday profit. Their names have been changed. Study them and do even better for yourself.

How Laid-Off Leo D. Was Led to Construct a Big-Selling Article

Fifty-two-year-old Leo D. had been working for thirty years and was still paying off the mortgage on his suburban home and sending his last two youngsters to college. He put in overtime now and then, and that helped. He looked forward to retiring in his sixties with his home paid off, his children established, and his grandchildren to enjoy. His youngest son was a problem, a "hippie," as they called them; but every family had problems. Leo didn't expect to get rich or famous, but he had provided his family with a comfortable home and good clothes and food, and had educated them all.

But hard times struck, and Leo was laid off indefinitely. He was shocked, but he would receive unemployment compensation for the next six months, if need be. He searched for work desperately, meanwhile, but landed nothing. Panic gripped him. How would he hang on to his home and send his children through college? He and Lois, his wife, trimmed their expenditures to the quick and even passed up their summer camping vacation.

But the comparatively small compensation would cease coming in before long, and he would have to exist on his savings! I taught Leo the secret mental power of profitable concentration. After learning it he triggered it with the Miracle Mind Magic

Stimulator, and it flashed into his conscious mind a simple invention for teen-age play. In a burst of inspired activity, fired with concentration, Leo manufactured it himself from inexpensive materials and advertised it for sale in the outdoor magazines. It was an instant hit.

In no time Leo was making a profit of about $700 a month, and the business was growing fast. Suddenly, he was called back to work and returned to it, under the persuasion of his wife. But he continued selling the article by mail, limiting the advertising to bring him only the business he could handle. Even then the demand for his product spread so widely and internationally that he fell weeks behind in filling his orders. Leo could have retired right then from his job.

*How Ashley C. Saved the Company He Worked
for and Was Rewarded with a Big Promotion*

The company which Ashley C. worked for as an engineer, and two others, were contracted by a giant corporation to complete developing a necessary engineering device for it. The three firms developed different versions of the device, and one of them (not Ashley's) won the contract to manufacture it for the giant corporation.

The loss dealt Ashley's company a staggering blow, and its employees were worried sick about losing their jobs. Ashley explained his alarming prospects to me, for he had a family and children to support, and a home to pay for. He insisted that he still had faith in his company's version of the device, but that the device still had some difficult problems to solve—problems that had lost his company the contract to manufacture it.

I persuaded Ashley to try to solve them with the secret mental power to concentrate profitably. He doubted if that could help. He and the capable engineers of his company had "sweated their brains out on it" and failed. But his plight was so desperate that he agreed to make the effort.

Ashley mastered the secret mental power fast and tried it. To his amazement, he though he suddenly found the much-wanted solution for the device. With the secret mental power to control others, he persuaded his tottering company to test it on a big scale, even without the backing of the giant concern! To his relief, his company was soon so satisfied with the test that it tooled up for production of a commercial version of the device, although no commercial market for it existed yet.

Months later the giant corporation reopened the bidding and increased, by several times, its order for the device. This time, thanks to Ashley's solution, his company's bid was significantly below that of the company that had won the contract previously. Ashley was handed a nice promotion and a startling increase in pay.

How a Boss-Harassed Personnel Manager Kept Employees His Company Wanted and Got Himself a Big Raise

Lester W. was a personnel manager and the big concern he worked for had a difficult time keeping employees it wanted. Its president regularly criticized Lester for not solving the problem, but Lester found it most complex. There were so many reasons why employees quit the place. When he tried to pin them down the reasons grew even more complex. But work fell back badly when such workers left, for they usually left during the busiest period of the year because demands for their skills were greatest then. Lester dreaded even going to his office, terrified that other wanted men were leaving and bringing down on him the increasing venom of his boss.

I advised Lester to learn the secret mental power of profitable concentration and apply it to his harrowing problem. He studied it and mastered it swiftly. He soon discovered, after applying the secret rules, that *"the little things"* not the big things, were often the reasons for the departures of the wanted men. He found, furthermore, that these irritations ranged all the way from the location of the parking lot to the use of a time clock. The time clock infuriated professional employees, like engineers and accountants, who felt degraded by it. They also resented being addressed by their Christian names when they had university degrees. There were also personality conflicts with supervisors.

Lester brought out these problems boldly to the wanted men who desired to leave. To his surprise he hit the nail on the head repeatedly and adjusted matters to please them. The employee turnover rate decreased remarkably. The president was so pleased with Lester that he rewarded him with a big raise in salary.

SUMMARY OF THIS SECRET MENTAL POWER

To concentrate profitably is to see in otherwise meaningless matter or phenomena something which others do not easily see, and to derive fantastic satisfaction (or even riches) from it. Acquire this secret mental power easily by following these simple routines:

1. Face the problem or situation which confounds you.
2. With the Miracle Mind Magic Stimulator trigger the right physiological language in you which puts you in the perfect mood for the keen, penetrating patience of profitable concentration.
3. Apply the sixteen simple secret rules for profitable concentration, and the seven rules for profitable research concentration if you need to research for it.
4. You will be stunned by the miracle of mind magic that will result—and the profits that will tumble into your lap.

Lesson 8

The Secret Mental Power
to Control Your
Nervous Tension and Worry

Nervous tension and worry divides you into a number of conflicting personalities, very much like a multiple personality, with each one pulling you in a different direction. It is worse than confused thinking because it leaves you unable to accept logic and common sense, even when these stare you in the face.

Unlike confused thinking, you *can* reason sensibly when afflicted with nervous tension and worry, but you are so unstable that you cannot stick to your premises, and your confidence in your ability to carry them through is so fleeting that you are soon no better off than you were before you reasoned them out. Even after you are zooming to your goal, dream, or wish, the smallest obstacle throws you off the track. You also tend to recollect failures more easily than successes, and grow pessimistic. Nervous tension and worry stimulate your fear-sympathetics and send your heart and breathing racing—so fast at times that you feel faint and short of breath. The least difficulty you encounter turns you jumpy; you perspire with a cold sweat and your knees feel weak. Your muscles hypertone fast, then undertone to the verge of flabby paralysis. You give way easily to tears, and tremble. You may be driven to contemplate suicide.

Such a wretched physiological language drives your hidden

powers into hiding. With the secret mental power to control nervous tension and worry you normalize this acquired physiological language and put your nervous tension and worry to flight. So, master well this secret mental power.

Profits You Can Realize from Controlling Nervous Tension and Worry

Some of the most incredible changes in people took place after they controlled their nervous tension and worry. People who seemed hopelessly afflicted with diseases like stomach ulcers were cured when they controlled their nervous tensions. Others, like severe stutterers and stammerers, who could hardly utter a few fluent words, changed into remarkable speakers and became world-wide leaders on their power of oratory (Sir Winston Churchill is but one example).

Paralyzed people, confined to wheel chairs for decades, rose to their feet and freed their pets in burning buildings and stumbled out behind them. Terror-stricken, impoverished widows entered the business world and accumulated wealth in surprisingly short time. Humiliated and dishonored people with "little to offer," bolted into the romantic field and won heiresses or Prince Charmings for lifetime mates. Handfuls of doomed soldiers charged, single-handed, into large bodies of enemy troops and carved trails of freedom through them. Feeble old women, accosted by armed, giant young criminals, turned on them with their purses and routed them. Shipwrecked men in ice-cold water swam remarkable distances for as much as three days to safety. Helplessly licked defendants "let go" against the prosecution and saved themselves.

There is practically nothing, no matter how incredible, that somebody has not achieved when he controlled his nervous tension and worry! Sixty-five percent of all warts, according to a noted dermatologist, disappear if the patient believes that a particular cure will work. A fifty-six-year-old man, after suffering a nervous breakdown following his financial ruin in a national depression, controlled it and came back to create a business encompassing 900 stores across the country.

What Happens in Your Body Due to Nervous Tension and Worry

When you are seized with nervous tension and worry you fall prey to something resembling an attack of anxiety neurosis. Your fear-sympathetics dominate you and you endure acute episodes of extreme fearfulness. These may consist of a feeling of impending doom, or even a fear of insanity, a fear of having a heart attack (for you suffer breathlessness), or of some other serious affliction. You might experience a smothering choking, or struggling to breathe, a sighing, a discomfort in the chest and a lump in the throat. You might suffer on and off from dizziness, faintness, weakness, fatigue, inward shakiness, tingling sensations in your skin, rapidly beating pulse, tremors, insomnia. "I feel very nervous and chest tight," one victim will claim. You go about with a feeling of great discomfiture, convinced (like a paranoid) that the whole world is against you and is trying to hold you down. You feel depressed and turn to anger and dread when you can't shake these oppressions loose. That tightens the cruel hold of your fear-sympathetics on you and tenses your muscles to the immobility point. You are tempted to grab things and throw them, to yell at the top of your voice, to shout every four-letter word you know, to destroy everything in sight, to free yourself from the bottled-up feeling.

The condition is initiated and prolonged by worry—endless worry about things you can do little about, except to complain to deaf ears. This leads to frustration in you and to the aggravation of the unhealthy physiological language that has erupted in you, until you border on hysteria.

Why Your Physiological Language of Fear Soon Develops into an Uncontrollable Habit

Your physiological language of fear develops into an uncontrollable habit when prolonged. Even if its causes disappear or are gotten rid of, your fear-sympathetics will have conditioned your heart to pump faster, your lungs to breathe more swiftly and more shallowly and leave you with a breathless sensation, your throat to tighten easily, your body to shake with tremors, and for you to stay awake in bed.

All this results in your muscles remaining chronically overtense. Even though they relax periodically, like the stammerer's throat muscles when he is silent, the moment you think or act again, like the moment the stammerer talks again, they overcontract and imprison you in a borderline neurosis. With the aid of your fear-conditioned, fear-activated body, they keep you on edge, so to speak, leaving you prone to lose your equanimity upon the least disturbance and to strike out, curse, or shout. By repressing yourself from doing so, you *increase* your feeling of frustration and retain its unhealthy physiological language.

This changes you from one type of person into another—or into one who is ruled by such an unhealthy physiological language *naturally*. Your fear-sympathetics dominate you completely now, and the harder you try to oust it, the stronger it holds you in its grasp. You have degenerated into a "nervous" person and a "chronic worrier."

How Your Acquired Physiological Language of Fear Alters Your Body Responses and Makes Those Changes Permanent

Your physiological language of fear makes its uncontrollable repsonses in you permanent by supersensitizing the brain centers of your heart, of your bronchi, of your blood vessels, and of all your skeletal muscles, to the least stimulus from your brain. A French physician believes that terrifying emotional experiences can trigger diabetes. Your physiological reactions to the least stimulation are, as a consequence, so violent that you break out easily into tremors. You become a *zombie of fear*! Fear is your king, ruler, and enslaver, through your bedeviled physiological language. It pulls the strings of your nerves and throws you into terror-action, like a marionette in the hands of its master!

How You Regularly Reverse the Physiological Habit of Pain in You

The amount of pain which one can endure varies from person to person. It depends upon your temperament, culture, past experience with any pain, expectation of the intensity of the pain, and your fear of danger. Due to differences in the presence and activity of their pain receptors, some people feel the same pain more than other people. On the average, though, most men and women possess the same neurological sensitivity to pain. But the *psychological* reaction to it *varies greatly*. Your conscious mind, in other words, controls the amount of pain you feel. That's why your pain tends to grow worse at night, when you have more time to think about it. That's why you feel it less, too, when you suffer from another discomfort at the same time.

That's why noise, which is a form of pain, has been used to reduce the reaction to the primary pain. Clenching the fists, wringing the hands, gripping a metal bar, stamping, talking fast, shouting, cursing, hopping around, leaping about wildly, and so forth, distract from the pain felt (or from the morbid dwelling of the conscious mind on it). That's why soldiers often don't feel their wounds on the battlefield and why boxers can fight with broken hands, noses, or jaws, and continue receiving murderous blows on those injured parts during the competition. But both of them wince the next day if someone just touches them lightly on those parts, for their conscious minds are then keenly aware of the expectant pain. In all such instances of feeling no pain, the physiological language of the individual is reversed from the normal one which *does* register the pain he feels, to one which *does not.* It is reversed each time either by his conscious mind *not thinking* about the pain (like the wounded soldier on the battlefield), or by his body doing something which distracts his conscious mind away from the pain (like clenching his fists).

The Magic of the Psycho-Feedback: The Strictly Mental Alpha High to Relax and Unwind You Anywhere, at any Time

The alpha state, according to physiologists, is an almost complete lack of anxiety and suggests that it might become a useful tranquilizer which may liberate thousands from chemical sedatives, hypnotics, and soporifics, and from the damaging and sometimes addicting side effects that accompany them. You don't have to risk suffering from the possible side effects of expensive electronic devices attached to your head to attain the relaxing state of the alpha high. Alpha waves emanate from your subconscious mind. They occur in the *inattentive* brain, such as during drowsiness or light sleep, or narcosis (that is, in the drugged or anesthetized state), or when the eyes are closed.

Alpha waves occur in mental states, in brief, in which the subconscious mind more or less takes over control of the brain. The alpha waves are abolished when visual and other types of stimulation influence the individual, or by mental effort (like mathematical calculation), or in other states in which the conscious mind is used actively. With the *psycho-feedback* you can attain this same feeling of serenity, detachment, and drifting, but yet of alertness (or of full *conscious mind control* of the alpha waves of the subconscious mind), which makes the state *unlike* drowsiness. You have then achieved a strictly "mental alpha high." *That* is the secret magic of the *psycho-feedback*. The psycho-feedback can be used *any time, anywhere,* for it requires no machine or device, no quiet or privacy, and carries no possible danger of electric shock or disturbance of the brain or nervous system. So, learn now how to create and use this tremendous magic tool of secret mental powers.

How to Control Your Nervous Tension and Worry Immediately with the Psycho-Feedback

First Step. Practice the magical psycho-feedback alone in your room. You will soon be able to use it any time, anywhere, to unwind your nerves in a flash. Drugs, tranquilizers, brain-wave machines and the like will, thereafter, be burdensome, expensive, perilous, and impractical for ready use.

To practice the psycho-feedback, sit down or rest comfortably. Lay your right palm flat against the left side of your chest, just below and against the bottom border of your left breast. (See Illustration 8-1.) Feel and listen to the speed and force of your heartbeat for about two or three minutes. Familiarize yourself with it, so you can detect instantly any marked alteration in its speed and force.

Keep your palm there and visualize an approaching situation in your life which is converting you into a nervous wreck. Vividly picture the situation and the persons involved in it. The person may be someone you want romantically (including your wife or

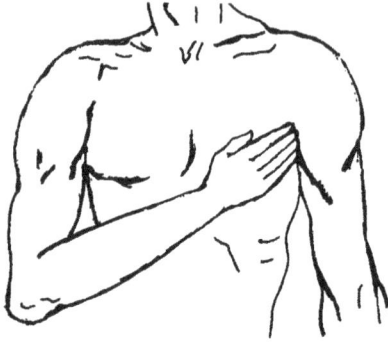

Illustration 8-1

husband). Or it may be your superior at work, a potential influential backer, a doctor to diagnose you, a lawyer to defend you, a prosecutor to prosecute you. Or the person and the environment together may constitute a serious threat, such as, a perilous journey to undertake, a contest to compete in, a contract to seek, a client to win, a bully to confront, a difficult customer to sell to, a new stock to buy, an inefficient subservient to discharge, an incorrigible to discipline, an important test to pass, a dangerous physical feat to attempt, a brain-cracking problem to solve.

Whatever it may be, imagine, in detail, *the very worst* that could befall you from the unavoidable confrontation. Envision, in other words, the person you want romantically spurning you in the most insulting manner; your superior at work condemning you most humiliatingly; your potential backer disdaining you with the utmost contempt; your doctor diagnosing you most fatally; your lawyer analyzing your case as hopeless; the prosecutor the harshest; the bully the toughest; the inefficient subservient to discharge, the gentlest and kindest soul; the incorrigible to discipline, the most dangerous blackguard; the perilous journey to undertake, the surest road to disaster; the contest to compete in, the surest to lose; the client, the most impossible to win; the customer, the most impossible to sell; the stock, the surest to lose money on; the important examination, the surest for you to fail; the physical feat, the surest you won't accomplish; the brain-cracking problem, the surest you won't solve.

Just imagine, *in detail, the very worst* that could befall you from that unavoidable confrontation. Note the speed of your heartbeat again. If you have *vividly* imagined the worst that could befall you in the situation, your heart will beat noticeably harder and faster. That is precisely what would happen to you in the actual situation. If your heart does not beat noticeably harder and faster than before, you have *not* imagined vividly enough the worst that could happen to you in that situation. Perhaps you are afraid to face it. But *face it now* when it can do you no harm! Force yourself to imagine it *at its worst*, until your heart beats decidedly harder and faster! Practice and do it (it won't take you long), and you'll be ready for the second step.

How to Control Your Nervous Tension and Worry Swiftly with the Psycho-Feedback

Second Step. In the first step you fill yourself with all the terror, rage, confusion, bewilderment, shock, and horror possible of the approaching situation. Your fear-sympathetics fire into you the full blast of their nerve-electricity and completely alter your normal physiological language. Your heart races (even if it doesn't pound your chest savagely), your breathing speeds up (even if you don't feel short of breath), the blood pours into your muscles, and your muscles hypertense with a murderous muscle tone. Your very brain feels as if it's pinching the top of your head and bristling the hairs there. You feel palpitations, cold sweats, faintness, weak knees.

Now, imagine that your heart is beating *normally again.* ("Beat" it *normally* in your thoughts. "Beat" it in your thoughts *slower and less forcibly than it is beating right then!*) Your heart *will* respond to your "thought beat," as has been proven by physiologists. (Check on it with your right palm, which still rests over your heart.) You have already "lived through" the dreadful situation, and it has drained your fear-sympathetics. So your heartbeat responds to your normal "thought beat" and beats quietly now. At once your breathing becomes lazy again, blood rushes from your muscles back to your skin and visceral organs, and your muscles relax and feel calm. Your physiological language has been normalized, for you realize that no worse can happen to you in that coming situation than what just "has." And yet, you are still alive and little the worse for wear.

To put it another way, you have imagined *the very worst* that could happen to you in that coming situation, and you have *fed it back to yourself thorough your conscious mind.* That is the psycho-feedback.

Why the Psycho-Feedback Gets Rid of Your Nervous Tension and Worry Quickly and Effectively

The attack of the psycho-feedback on your nervous tension and worry is incomparable, because suppression bottles up fear and anger within you to the degree where you magnify them into uncontrollable terror and rage. These diabolical emotions throw your physiological language into chaos. That chaos feeds itself back to your brain through your sensory nerves, and you suppress it with your conscious mind, because you are still afraid of the threatening situation. From your conscious mind the chaos burrows itself into your subconscious mind and converts you into a chronic victim of its fear-sympathetics.

With the psycho-feedback, however, your conscious mind "kicks out" this suppressed chaos from *both* of your minds. That normalizes your physiological language promptly, and your nervous tension and worry over the coming situation vanishes. You can kick out such a suppressed chaos from *any and every* frightening situation you are about to experience with the psycho-feedback, and rid yourself of the nervous tension and worry it brings you *in no time.* And you can repeat the psycho-feedback any time, anywhere, as many times as you wish, to unwind and relax you with the strictly mental alpha high. And it won't cost you a penny, discomfit you, or require burdensome equipment which can be used only in certain places, much less endanger you with possible side effects.

The Miracle of the "Thought Beat"

Any time you face *any* situation thereafter that makes you nervous and worries you unduly, either lay your palm flat, below your left breast (or gently clasp your left wrist with your right hand and listen to your heart beat. (See Illustration 8-2.) Then

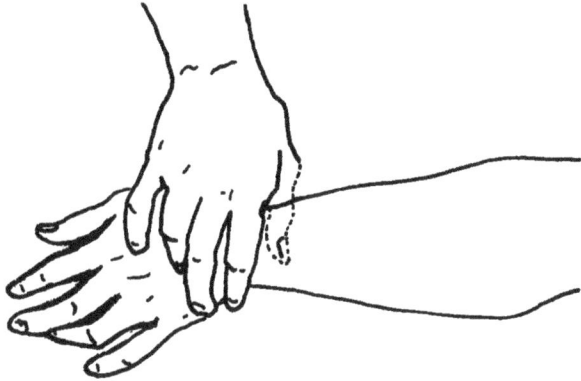

Illustration 8-2

With the inner part of the second knuckle of your
right thumb, feel your pulse beat on the inner third
of the bottom of your left wrist (or of your right
wrist if you prefer). Can be done standing or sitting.

"thought beat" your heart back to its normal pace, which you
recognize from your practice of the psycho-feedback. (Physiologists have had subjects slow their hearts down markedly in the
laboratory simply by having them watch their heartbeats being
recorded and *thinking them* into slowing down. The same
principle operates with the miracle of the "thought beat," except
that you can apply it *any time, anywhere.)*

Note: With further practice you won't even have to lay your
right palm across your left chest. Just train yourself to duplicate
your normal heartbeat in your thoughts at any time, by practicing
that alone. Then, any time you feel nervous or start worrying, you
automatically know that your heart *is* beating much faster (and
harder) than normal. To slow it back down to normal and restore
your normal physiological language, just duplicate your normal
heartbeat in your thoughts and vividly envision your heart slowing
down swiftly to that pace. Your heart will do so, just as it does in
the laboratory.

Below are case histories of some of those who used the secret
mental power to control their nervous tensions and worries swiftly
for everyday profit. Their names have been obviously changed.
Study them well and do even better yourself in similar situations.

How Hesitant Jack M. Turned into a Rousing Speaker in an Instant

Jack M. was intelligent and full of ideas, but he could hold no one's interest for long, socially or in business, because of his nervous tension. It would seize him when he least expected and divest him of his confidence. It filled him with anxiety and confused his thinking. Whatever he said thereafter was hardly worth listening to, for he became uncertain of himself and fearful of taking a bold stand in anything. Others either ignored him then or took their departures. Jack grew supersensitive to such treatment, and his deplorable condition became worse.

I explained to him that his nervous tension forced his body to speak a handicapping physiological language, and I taught him the secret of the psycho-feedback. With it he "lived through" the most humilating experience he could suffer from *any* social or business experience in which he failed. That quickly normalized his physiological language and banished his nervous tension whenever he spoke. He regained his lost confidence and turned instantly into a convincing speaker.

How Stanley V. Subdued His Ulcers

Stanley V. had suffered for years from stomach ulcers. Doctor after doctor treated him, with little success. It was finally blamed on "psychic causes." A psychiatrist helped him then, but told him outright that he had a tendency to worry too much, that he had to conquer that tendency.

I described to Stanley how that tendency had altered his normal physiological language into an abnormal one by putting it under the dominance of his fear-sympathetics. His fear-sympathetics drew the blood out of his digestive system and poured it into his muscles, leaving the lining of his stomach with insufficient blood to function healthily. That caused it to break out into ulcers because it deprived his stomach of its normal amount of nutrition and of its normal waste removal. Stanley had to restore his physiological language to normal, so the lining of his stomach could be supplied again with the normal amount of blood.

To achieve that, I taught him how to meet every situation

that made him worry with the psycho-feedback. Stanley mastered the psycho-feedback in no time. With it he restored his badly disturbed physiological language back to normal, and his digestion improved remarkably very soon.

How Marcia L. Controlled Her "Nerves" by
Lowering Her Heart Rate with a Compelling
Picture-Thought

Marcia L. was not a beauty, and she worried unnecessarily about it. The office where she worked was crowded with "young chicks," as she put it, and she felt that she no longer rated highly with her impressionable boss. The young chicks, Marcia complained bitterly to me, got raises faster than she, although her work outranked theirs. They were also assigned simpler tasks than she, which increased her responsibilities without the rewards. As a result, she detested her boss and the young chicks. But that was to no avail, she confessed, for it turned her into a bundle of nerves. She had tried self-hypnosis, and was resorting to tranquilizers and was suffering from side effects—all without lasting improvement.

I explained to Marcia how the unfair situation had aroused her fear-anger-sympathetics and had altered her normal physiological language into an explosive one. I taught her the psycho-feedback and had her imagine *the very worst thing* that could happen to her at the office, and to "live through" it so vividly that she exhausted herself.

· Marcia did so, and promptly controlled her nervous tension and worry every day by "thought beating" her racing heart back down to normal speed whenever she felt her nervous tension returning. After that, the situation no longer affected her seriously because she had already "lived through" it. So she accepted the fact that there was no such thing as absolute justice in anything. She realized, too, that those "young chicks" would not remain young forever. Younger ones would be employed there before long and be favored over *them*. Life was life, and no one could change every aspect of it. Marcia's heart beat slower again regularly, and her physiological language spoke normally in a permanent manner. She got rid of her "nerves" and enjoyed life again. Not only that, but her boss started showing her far more consideration, due to her new attitude and personality, and she got an excellent, unexpected raise in salary!

SUMMARY OF THIS SECRET MENTAL POWER

Controlling your nervous tension and worry changes you from an ineffectual, indecisive person into a boldly acting, commanding one who achieves his goals, dreams, or wishes with surprising ease. To acquire this secret mental power most easily, follow these simple routines:

1. Face the fear, dread, or threatening calamity which fills you with nervous tension and worry.
2. Understand how it changes your physiological language by arousing the symptoms of your fear-sympathetics (which resemble those of anxiety neurosis).
3. Oust this ruinous physiological language from you with the magic of the psycho-feedback and keep it under control by maintaining your heart rate normal with the miraculous "thought beat."
4. You will be freed of nervous tension and worry speedily because these states cannot enslave you unless they can change your physiological language.

Lesson 9

The Secret Mental Power to Protect Yourself from Domination by Others

When you are under the domination of others you degenerate into something less than a complete person. You become then just so much of yourself and no more, for your dominator divests you of the most independent part of yourself. He converts you into a divided personality, with the most aggressive side of you imprisoned in his shackles, and the most submissive side of you allowed to go free. And so, you stumble about like a much inferior person than you actually are. You are like a genius being compelled to live and act like a moron, until he is convinced that he *is* one.

When you are dominated by someone, your best thinking and behavior are submerged and allowed to rise back only to the level to which your dominator will permit. Your whole make-up is enslaved to his whims and fancies and is subservient to his moods. Since he will consider you only as a good-natured robot with half the intelligence *he* has, he treats you like one and *converts* you into such a creature because your physiological language attunes itself to that state. Hence, you evolve into one psychologically, and your physiological language accepts such a change as your permanent one. Your goals, dreams, or wishes give way to your dominator's goals, dreams, or wishes, and you wilt away into little better than a helpless nonentity.

Profits You Can Realize by Protecting
Yourself from Domination by Others

The profits which certain people gained by protecting themselves from domination by others are beyond description. Many such people tore themselves free from overbearing persons who squeezed every drop of personality out of them. Others freed themselves from the lack of consideration of "work-horse" bosses. Others ripped loose from neighbors or "friends" who tried to force them to be nobodies and keep them down socially or romantically. Others threw over careers they disliked, despite the derision of their family, friends, or associates, and leaped into the ones they preferred and zoomed to the top, like magic. Others sought mates whom they had been assured they could never win, and won them with ease! Many retired long before they were "supposed to" and lived, at last, as they always wanted to.

Each of them had his own goal, dream, or wish, but could not achieve it because someone dominated him (or her) and held him back from it. Once he broke the enslaving chain, though, he either skyrocketed upward in his career, or attained a joy in living which he did not believe possible. Do likewise for yourself with this secret mental power.

What Happens in Your Mind When You Are
Dominated by Someone

When you are dominated by another person you change into an entirely different person than you are naturally. You are filled with uncertainties, fears, and repressions, because you no longer act freely. You can't make a move or a decision without the approval of your dominator. You go through this undermining ritual so repeatedly with him that your conscious mind is conditioned to thinking like that not only with him, but with *everything else you do*! It becomes your *habit of thinking*!

The neurons in your brain, as a result, form fixed codes of doubt, fear, uncertainty and, finally, of terror. And, try as you might, you can't shake those codes loose. The harder you try to, indeed, the more firmly they settle into those devastating combinations, because the more you fail to escape from anyone's domination, the more apprehensive you become. In time, you stay awake nights dreading the horror of more humiliating domination. Abnormal quantities of waste products accumulate in your brain tissues and deprive them of needed oxygen and nourishment. That aggravates your already morbid state of mind and plagues you, when you arise in the morning, with the vague sensation of a hangover. You reach the point where you feel like attacking the "hateful" person and running away. But you don't dare. And yet, you don't know how you can continue enduring him.

What Happens to Your Actions and Behavior When You Are Dominated by Someone

With your mind dominated so crushingly by another person, your actions (which are directed by your mind) go off half-cocked. You no longer do things calmly and enjoyably, but laboriously and spasmodically. You hate to get up in the morning, much less go to work. You dread to meet anybody you might have to greet or converse with, for you don't know how you'll impress him. Your natural personality has been squashed out of you so thoroughly that you feel like the most inferior and degraded creature on earth.

You expect a look of respect from nobody, much less a pleasant "howdy." So, you try to avoid everybody and escape the embarrassment of being snubbed, or of being greeted "peculiarly," or of being glanced at as an "odd-ball," a "crack-pot," a "queer duck," a "freak." That little encounter, even though brief, would rankle you additionally all day long and add to the misery which awaits you again from your dominator. If the dominating occurs at home, you will be a wreck before you even step out of the house.

At work you make more mistakes than before, get along less well, are bypassed more by the friendly and heckled more by the derisive. Your temper flares quickly, or you have to struggle to keep it under control. Your speech becomes hasty and impatient with your equals, and defiant or submissive with your superiors. You are too conscientious and hard-striving, though, to be fired. Your dominator might even relish keeping you there to kick you around and rid himself of his "brutality complex." You, as a result, degenerate into a borderline hysteric.

What Happens to Your Physiological
Language When You Are Dominated by Someone

Your mind, your actions and behavior are so drastically changed when you are dominated by another person that your physiological language undergoes a traumatic alteration. Your sympathetics then flash into you repeatedly both fight and flight commands, with one swiftly succeeding the other, or warring against the other, or blasting you into action in their endless degrees of combinations.

The very thought of your dominator fills you now with terror of him, and later with fury against him. Later still it impels you both to flee from him and to confront him at the same time, and leaves you struggling, panic-stricken, with those oppositely-pulling forces, to the point of action paralysis. Your pupils dilate, your face turns pale, you feel a lump in your throat, your stomach flutters, your breathing becomes swift and shallow, you lose your appetite, you tremble easily, and you feel weak and faint because your heart beats fast, but feebly. You can neither fight nor flee from the oppressive situation, but have to face it like a helpless prisoner strapped for the guillotine. Your body is speaking a physiological language that annihilates you as a person! You have truly degenerated into a "weak-kneed" creature; into the "coward," the "yellow guts," the "jellyfish."

The Secret Clench-and-Relax to Protect You
Against Being Dominated by Others

The best way to protect yourself against being dominated by others is by halting at once the resulting physiological language alteration that takes place in you due to the fight-or-flight sympathetics' grip that seizes you. Depending upon how crushing the affront to you is, you will then frown (as your pupils dilate), your muscles will tense (with fighting muscle tone), a lump will form in your throat (as your throat muscles overcontract), your heart will pound faster and harder, and your chest will feel congested from it and from your shallow, faster breathing. Your stomach will flutter a little, your leg muscles will shudder slightly, and your mouth will become "dry" (as your salivary glands secrete less). Even your fists will clench wholly or partially, automatically.

The Clench-and-Relax Program

To halt this new, unhealthy physiological language from altering your natural personality, you have to abort the above resulting changes which it brings about in your body. You then regain your normal physiological language, which is ruled by a balanced sympathetic-parasympathetic influence. Do so easily with the secret Clench and Relax. Practice and master its five easy steps, described below. Do them while standing.

1. Clench your arms (and fists) and legs as hard as you can, for exactly two seconds. (This lets your arm and leg muscles 'attack" your detestable dominator.)
2. Then relax them completely for four seconds.
3. If you still feel "upset" by your dominator, repeat steps 1 and 2.
4. Your attacking muscles will lose their fighting muscle tone, and your sympathetics will be fooled into "thinking" that you have "lambasted" that person and will cease their pugnacious commands to your muscles to "beat him up." Your body will respond to the change in commands, and your physiological language will normalize.
5. Your whole body will dispatch messages of normalcy to your conscious mind, and your conscious mind will tear loose from the imprisoning grip of your dominator over you.

That, as simple as it seems, is the fantastically effective Clench and Relax.

Below are case histories of some of those who used the secret mental power to protect them from domination by others for typical everyday gain. Study them well and do even better for yourself in similar situations or circumstances.

How Trampled-Down Harry S. Aroused the Keen
Respect of His Overbearing Superiors

By nature Harry S. was a gentle, kind-hearted soul who went out of his way to please others. He was even more so where he worked.

But his efforts brought out the worst from some of his minor and major bosses. They decided that Harry *was* inferior to them, or he wouldn't be trying so hard to please. So they treated him like a nobody and hardly listened to what he said. They promoted others, without his talents, faster than he was promoted. Harry brooded over that and it altered his normal physiological language. His heartbeat and breathing speeded up easily at work and remained speeded up for hours. His muscles readily became "jumpy" and caused him to make unnecessary errors that brought caustic remarks from his overbearing superiors. Harry got worse and worse as his physiological language "spoke" more heatedly.

I taught him the secret mental power to protect himself from domination by others. Being so desperate, he learned it swiftly. Whenever he confronted a superior thereafter, he normalized his tempestuous physiological language with the Clench and Relax, slowed down his heartbeat and breathing, and relaxed his tensed-up muscles. He conducted himself with his bosses with calmness and dignity thereafter. One overbearing superior after another gained respect for him at once and treated him like an important employee. Harry started advancing surprisingly fast in the company.

How Donna M. Freed Herself from a Devilish
Love Enslavement, and Married a Man Who
Adored Her

Donna M. was widowed young, and worked hard and lived alone ever since. At fifty-two she met Lance A., a lady's man many years her junior. He dominated her for six long years with his jaunty romantic airs and took red-handed advantage of her. He promised her marriage, but only bled her for sizable loans which he never repaid. He even inveigled her into buying him a luxurious automobile with her hard-earned savings. Donna realized that he was making a fool of her and would probably never marry her. But she could not free herself of him.

Weeping frantically, she confessed her problem to me. To dominate her, I explained to her, Lance had altered her into a different person than she was naturally. She was filled now with dread and uncertainty because she could make no independent move unless it pleased Lance. That changed her physiological language into a self-annihilating one.

So I taught her the secret mental power to protect her from domination by others. In despair, she mastered it fast. Every time she thought of or dealt with Lance thereafter, she protected herself against his influence with the Clench and Relax. When Lance perceived that he was losing his hold over her, he showed his true colors and became insulting. That cut Donna to the quick, and she broke loose at last and severed relations with him. Lance tried repeatedly later to make amends, but Donna again protected herself against him with the Clench and Relax.

Six months later she met a charming man of her own age. They were married in six months, adopted a ten-year old girl, and are living a life of bliss.

How Elmer T., on the Verge of Legal Catastrophe, Recalled Neglected but Vital Evidence Suddenly and Won His Freedom

Elmer was worried sick about the case against him. He was not guilty as charged, but the evidence against him was so misleading that he was made to appear guilty. The prosecutor bore down on him so domineeringly that Elmer could hardly think straight. Terror-stricken, he recalled the secret mental power to protect him from domination, which I had taught him to use at work.

With the secret Clench and Relax he normalized his delirious physiological language. (Since he was seated in the witness chair he had to turn his toes upward hard to contract his calf muscles, and to press his knees together hard to contract his thighs sufficiently.) The throbbing left his chest and head, and he became calm enough to think clearly again. When the prosecutor pounced upon him once more, Elmer listed to him carefully and thought deeply before answering him. To his amazement, the neglected but vital evidence he needed flashed into his mind and he blurted it out. The prosecutor blinked. Elmer had turned the tide of defeat into victory.

SUMMARY OF THIS SECRET MENTAL POWER

To protect yourself from domination by others is an unbeatable secret mental power to free you from people who try to flatten you into a nonentity, to take outlandish advantage of you, to spitefully humiliate you, to make you look ridiculous to your friends or associates, or to crush you in your career. To acquire it most easily, follow these simple routines:

1. Once you are aware that your dominator has disordered your normal physiological language by hurting your feelings, embarrassing you, or what not,
2. Do the Clench and Relax program.
3. It will normalize your physiological language again.
4. You can then swiftly oust your dominator's influence over you from your mind and command his respect.

Lesson 10

Your Secret Mental Power to Gain Swift Control Over Others

When you gain swift control over others you attain your goals, dreams, or wishes with them or through them with magical speed and effectiveness. You are spared the long period of winning their confidence through logic or conviction, or through overcoming the influences of their advisors or associates. You are spared considerable doubt and anxiety in fitting them into the mold you want them in. (You are expected, of course, to use this secret mental power for worthy purposes only.) You then make them "see" what you see, not only mentally, but even physically, to a marked degree. An ignored homely woman, for example, can force an attractive man to "see" her as being a ravishing beauty physically when she gains swift control over him. So can a salesman make a prospective client "see" previously undetected value in his product; a physician make a grave patient "see" improvement in his condition.

Dishonestly, with that same power, a lazy worker can make his superior "see" him as industrious; a beggar can make his donor feel indebted to *him*; a swindler can make his victim feel grateful to him; a gold-digger wife can make her husband think she is wild about him; a social climber can make society people proud to be seen in *his* company; an aging man can make a fascinating young woman "see" him as much younger and intriguingly romantic, and so forth. When you control others swiftly, in other words, you acquire something for nothing, for you acquire from them something you have not earned and probably don't deserve. Without their even suspecting it, you enslave them to you and, whether they wish to or not, they do your bidding without realizing why. And you don't even have to command them to do so; they just do so unwittingly. They relish obeying you and feel delighted for having done so. When you use this secret mental power for a worthy purpose, you really bend people around your fingers. This secret mental power converts you into an unsuspected "slave owner" of free men. That's why you are expected to use it honorably.

The Fantastic Profits Gained from Swift Control Over Others

The profits which certain people reaped from swift control over others are truly fantastic. With it they made others give in to their persuasions or obey their commands, and drew out of them great capacities, unbelievable physical powers, or incredible talents which blessed both of them with mutual large gains.

With it such people freed others from ruinous bad habits, set vacillating people on goals that brought them security and satisfaction, and convinced others (like their grown children or relatives) to pursue rewarding careers that superficially appeared boring or grasping. They gained the support of those who impeded their advancements, gained the fealty and allegiance of rebellious mates, induced the hesitant to trade or negotiate with them, and made those who avoided them socially hunger after them. They reaped astoundingly in every phase of life. Do likewise and carve out a soft berth for yourself on earth, using the efforts and abilities of others. That's why it is short-sighted to plan to use this secret mental power unworthily, for you can profit far more by using it worthily.

How Others Resist Your Efforts to Control Them

It is obvious that other people won't automatically let you control them as you wish. Everybody dislikes being changed into a creature foreign to his nature. Everybody differs widely in brain structure from other people, and possesses a pattern of mental attitudes or potentialities which is distinctive to himself alone. As the psychologists assert, there are at least forty ways we can be clever with our minds. Everybody possesses his own color vision, and what another person sees in color is not identical to what *you* see. His very taste sensations differ from yours.

Even "normal" people may respond very differently to such substances as sugar, hydrochloric acid, salt, and so on. As the late Dr. Blakeslee summed it up, "Different people live in different worlds." At least, as far as their receiving impressions of the outer world is concerned. Even the speed and force of another person's heartbeat when he is relaxed and asleep differ from yours. Consequently, whenever you try to control anyone, his different mental built-in codes and his physiological language will resist you because they differ from yours, and will not conform readily to what you impose upon them.

The Obstacles You Face in Trying to Control Others

The important obstacles which you face in trying to control someone (or to change his mental built-in codes and his physiological language) consist of his lifetime habits of thinking, living, behaving, and body functioning. The very first look or word you two exchange already emphasizes that difference to him, for he puts his own personal interpretation on it. He might misinterpret it because *he* is still *he*, and he will therefore interpret everything he experiences according to how he imagines he understands it. So, at the very first look or word you two exchange, Joe (or Jane) might either elevate you or degrade you. Either way, you already have a hurdle to overcome in your path to control him. Even if you feel that he elevates you above himself, how do you know in *what* way? After you associate with him, too, even if briefly, he might grow disillusioned with you.

The longer he associates with you, in any event, the more his conclusions about you become altered. Some of his conclusions about you sink more deeply into him then, too, no matter if they are erroneous or based upon hearsay, acquired prejudice or superstition; while some other of his conclusions remain subject to change. He has "typed" you, in other words. His mind builds in codes formed from his "on-sight" conclusions about you, as well as from the conclusions he has arrived at about you through associating with you. His physiological language toward you, as a result, alters to conform to them, no matter how faintly. All of which adds more obstacles to your prospects of controlling him swiftly.

How to Soften Someone's Resistance to Your Controlling Him Swiftly

The more you try to control a person, the more stubbornly his built-in mental codes about you and his acquired physiological language toward you resist you. So, you have to soften him up first to your attempts.

To do so, give him no further reason for resisting you. Achieve that by making him feel super-comfortable with you. Let him feel that from you he has no reason to envy, beware of, guard against, turn aloof from, covet, flee from, differ with, rage against, dispute with, or hide from you. Let him feel that *you* bring him a breath of spring in this oppressive, distrustful, competitive, tension-filled, disillusioning, frustrating, generally pessimistic world, and that you will gladly "absorb" all worries from his mind and leave him relieved and refreshed. Don't become his catch-all, but let him feel that he can confide in you!

To achieve that miracle swiftly, the moment you lay eyes on him:

1. Forget yourself *entirely.* You will become self-conscious otherwise, and that erects a psychological wall between you two.
2. Then think of *him* alone! Think of him as being *the greatest person on earth—the very person* you are *most anxious to see and know.*

Your *para*sympathetic nervous system will gain the ascendancy in you and alter *your* physiological language into that of a person who genuinely feels that way about him. Your heart then beats like his, your glands secrete like his, your lungs breathe like his, your cheeks glow like his, and your voice, your movements, your posture, and the conclusions of your conscious mind ape his. The right things to say to him will dance upon your tongue and you *become* that person. That person swiftly accepts you as being that person, and softens toward you.

How to Convert a Person into Your Physiologically-Synchronizing Twin

This person now loses his built-in mental codes which resist your swiftly controlling him. But his subconscious mind still retains the tendency to trigger his resisting physiological language toward you. That compels you to soften totally his resistance to your control and make his body speak *your* physiological language back to you, and none other!

To achieve that, make *him* feel as eager to meet and talk to *you* as *you* have made yourself feel toward *him.* You want his *para*sympathetics, in other words, to dominate him to the degree where he harmonizes with you in heartbeat, glandular flow, body movement, and thinking, so that you two are converted into *physiologically-synchronizing twins.* That person will then acquire an irresistible affinity with you in anything you think or do, for he will be "speaking" your physiological language!

How to Condition Your Parasympathetic Nervous System

To do so, stop reminding yourself, first of all, that you are *not* really the person into whom you have changed yourself at the sight of him; that, actually, you are too uncertain of yourself to step forth and meet him on your own. If you don't stop doing that, *your own acquired physiological language* will alter back to what it was, and your heartbeat and breathing will speed up, your eyes will become evasive, your cheeks will pale, your body movements will become wary, and your conscious mind will fill with dread of that man or woman. That person will promptly detect something peculiar about you, and his own physiological language will alter back into one of anger and distrust of you.

Second, breathe more slowly and deeply now for at least five seconds, to overoxygenate your blood and discourage any tendency of your heartbeat and breathing to speed up. At the same time, *halt all introspection that flashes through your brain* and forcibly reflect only over the imagined delights of meeting that person again. Practice this in your room, alone, by visualizing a delicious dish and transposing the resulting ecstasy to your subject person, and "feel" the joy of meeting him spread through your cheeks. Compel yourself to experience this feeling so sharply that it pulls your cheeks apart into an infectious smile!

This "cheek-stimulus" (buccal stimulus) is a parasympathetic nervous system exciter because your parasympathetics fill your cheeks with blood when you blush. Your parasympathetics, as a consequence, will remain dominating you, your heartbeat and breathing will not speed up, and your body movements will retain the actions of your new self. The other person, despite himself or herself, will be converted into your physiologically-synchronizing twin.

How to Trigger Your Control Over Others with the Miracle Mind Magic Stimulator

Your great difficulty in using the secret mental power to control others is your constant awareness that you have to change yourself first into a different kind of person than you are naturally. The Miracle Mind Magic Stimulator will end that difficulty. How to practice and master it follows.

How to Proceed to Control Anyone

Sit alone in your room and visualize the person as you know him. Envision yourself meeting him (or her), with you being the most enchanting person he (or she) has ever met. (*That* is your goal, dream, or wish with this secret mental power.) Hold that vision in your mind for five seconds.

Now visualize yourself changing completely into that "most enchanting person." Visualize yourself thinking like him, gazing like him, smiling like him, speaking like him, moving and walking like him, gesturing like him, breathing confidently like him, reacting like him—becoming, in other words, *him* (or *her*, if you are a woman). Maintain this vision for four seconds.

Repeat that procedure three times, as you learned from practicing the Miracle Mind Magic Stimulator in Lesson 3. Intensify it each time, so you actually *feel yourself change* into *that most compelling person of all time.* Feel the very hairs on the middle-top of your head tingle with that all-conquering sensation, and feel your face and body radiate the energizing infrared rays which are flashed through your pores by the resulting dynamic tissue metabolism of such a dominating conception of yourself. Practice charging yourself with this "most irresistible person" feeling until you need to visualize it *but once* to alter your whole physiological language into that of such a person. You will be ready to use the secret mental power to control others swiftly.

Below are case histories of some of those who used this secret mental power to control others swiftly for everyday profit. The names have been changed. Study the cases well and do still better yourself in your own situations.

How Homely, Middle-Aged, Ignored Sarah P.
Made an Attractive $70,000-a-Year Man See
Her as a Ravishing Young Beauty

At fifty-four, Sarah P. had been widowed three years. Her children had grown up and married and had their own families, and Sarah refused to be relegated, as she put it, into the role of the "old, baby-sitting grandma" and nothing more. She felt that she still had a more exciting life of her own to live.

The president of her company was a widower. He was tall, handsome, attractive with graying temples, and earned $70,000 a year. Sarah secretly wished to marry him. What a wonderful life she would live thereafter, she thought.

But she scoffed at the prospect. At her prettiest (and she had always been homely) she had captured only a typical working man as a spouse. Now, thirty-six years later, she also had bulky hips, heavy ankles, and the all-over look of aging. Yet, she revolted against the idea that life had passed her by.

She was deep in misery when she saw me. She hated her humdrum job and her dull life ahead. "What was I born for?" she cried. "Might as well kill myself! I've only lived like a beast of burden!"

Since she was obviously enamored with her company president, I taught her the secret mental power to gain swift control over others. With the Miracle Mind Magic Stimulator she promptly changed her frustrated physiological language into that of a ravishing young beauty. She then thought like such a woman, moved like her, smiled like her, spoke like her, gestured like her, breathed confidently like her, reacted like her. She became, in other words, *her.*

Then she started changing the president's built-in codes and his physiological language, and converted him into her physiologically-synchronizing twin.

He was her slave thereafter. He eagerly asked her for a date and, in the midst of it, described her as if she *were* a ravishing young beauty *who resembled the one she had changed herself into*! By the third date he fitted an engagement ring around her finger and whispered about the great touring honeymoon he had planned for them.

How Robert P., Socially a Nobody, Became
the Social Rage in an Instant

Robert P. was tired of being virtually a social outcast. At first he consoled himself by being glad to be left alone. "There is nothing like privacy!" he bragged, and found refuge in reading paperbacks and watching TV. Other people were so difficult to please, he concluded, that they were not worth the effort it took to impress them. It was simpler to be alone with his own interests, pets, or hobbies. Now and then he had a "buddy" or two, but they either married, moved away, or found different interests, and Robert wound up alone again. But he could no longer fight off his loneliness. Whenever he tried to join a social bunch, however, he experienced no success. He just couldn't hold people to him, he sighed in disgust.

I taught him the secret mental power to gain swift control over others. He yearned to join a particular social group, he confessed, but it didn't appear to want him.

With the Miracle Mind Magic Stimulator Robert changed his physiological language into that of an extraordinarily popular person. Then he thought like such a person, moved and walked like him, gestured like him, breathed confidently like him, reacted like him. He became, in other words, *him.*

This time he promptly changed the built-in codes of the different members of the bunch and converted them all into his physiologically-synchronizing twins. He was soon welcomed into their midst and was lionized both by the men and the women.

How Jack R. Made All the Associates Who Disagreed with His Idea Support It to the Hilt and Select Him as Their Leader

Jack R. was full of ideas, but the others in the firm failed to discern their possibilities. Jack became frustrated and resentful. Others with ideas inferior to his were favored and rewarded with big raises and promotions, while he was in danger of being laid off because he contributed "so little" to the company.

Jack told me that he could not convince his associates to put his ideas to the test. His ideas were new and unusual, and beyond the scope of their imaginations.

I taught him the secret mental power to gain swift control over others. With the Miracle Mind Magic Stimulator Jack changed his physiological language into that of a man who entranced others with his ideas, no matter how fantastic they sounded. He then thought like such a person, walked like him, smiled like him, spoke like him, gestured like him, breathed like him, reacted like him. He became, in other words, *him.*

To soften his associates' resistance to his idea, Jack forgot himself completely and thought of them as being *the greatest persons on earth*—the very persons he was *most anxious to please.*

That changed their built-in codes and converted them into his physiologically-synchronizing twins. They fell into the mood of Jack's thinking and speaking and agreed, to a man, with his idea. They tried it out and it went over big. They selected Jack as their idea leader thereafter and he was soon in line for a big post with the company.

How Helen G. Was Perceived as a Fascinating "Young Woman" Well Past Middle Age

Helen G. was a widow near sixty. Her children were grown up and married and had their own families, and she felt alone and abandoned. She worked all week and sat in the various get-together clubs on Saturday nights. But with the numbers of attractive and much younger women (especially divorcees and bachelorettes) to choose from, her romantic competition was overwhelming. Helen, nevertheless, refused to accept the role of a castoff. She still had many years ahead to live, she thought, but she dreaded passing them in abandoned loneliness and pining over her lost youth. She was no less capable of pleasing than she ever was, but most men seemed to pursue the younger women. Helen grieved over the injustice of their inclinations and condemned their "stupidity."

I taught her the secret mental power to gain swift control over others. She practiced it feverishly and felt a remarkable change overtake her as her half-mad physiological language normalized itself. Her heartbeat and breathing slowed, her muscles lost their anxious tension, her face relaxed, and a "promise" entered her eyes. She felt as if a big weight had fallen off her shoulders, and she acted—and appeared—many years younger. Best of all, she suggested a full capacity to thrill and excite.

Helen returned to the club. A desirable man of fifty-eight, whom she had secretly pined for but who had ignored her, approached her table and introduced himself. He was most attentive to her all evening, drove her home, and begged for a "date." They were married five months later. Helen could hardly believe that her much-wanted dream had come true so quickly and easily.

SUMMARY OF THIS SECRET MENTAL POWER

When you acquire swift control over others, you enslave them to you because they obey you implicitly and are molded by you, whether they like it or not. They put you on a pedestal without their suspecting why, and strain themselves to satisfy you. That's why this secret mental power has to be used for worthy purposes only. To acquire it swiftly, follow these simple routines:

1. Be aware of the fact that others will resist your efforts to control them, and realize what these obstacles are.
2. Realize, too, that people's resistance to your controlling them will grow with your efforts to do so.
3. First soften people's resistance to your swift control.

4. Then convert them into your physiologically-behaving twins.
5. To overcome your great difficulty in using this secret mental power, do the Miracle Mind Magic Stimulator the moment you see the person you want to control swiftly.

Lesson 11

Your Secret Mental Power to Enthrall Friends or Enemies

When you can enthrall your friends and your enemies, you will automatically rise over most of the barriers to your happiness you encounter on this earth. Without this secret mental power your life degenerates into a hard and unsatisfactory one. When your friends help you without limitation, they provide you with a springboard to leap to the realization of your goals, dreams, or wishes, with much less effort. When your *enemies* help you, in addition, the barriers in your way to these goals, dreams, or wishes vanish like smoke into thin air. To achieve by yourself alone what you can with the help of your friends and enemies is as impossible as it is for a lone Congressman to get a law passed by Congress without the help of other Congressmen.

The aid of your friends and enemies doesn't merely better your chances of realizing your goals, wishes, or dreams, but *multiplies* it. In a great many cases it even *guarantees* it! Some of your friends might know more about the specific details of the barriers in your way, while other friends might even have connections with people who can "lift" you over the barriers. If your enemies, on the other hand, are preventing you from climbing over the barriers, to enthrall them is to facilitate instantly your clearing the barriers. You might waste your whole lifetime, otherwise, in vain efforts to climb over those same barriers and end up sour, dejected, frustrated, insufferably pessimistic, bitterly envious of others with "half" your talents or abilities, who achieve those very goals of yours with the utmost ease. Just to have friends is not enough. You have to *enthrall* people to receive their utmost help. Your enemies, of course, have to be truly enthralled before they'll do anything for you.

The Fantastic Profits from Enthralling Friends or Enemies

The profits from enthralling friends or enemies are almost beyond adequate description. With this secret mental power, unpopular politicians gained office over seemingly insuperable opposition. The despised accused won their freedom. Derided young scientists received enviable honors and acclaim. Expelled students gained readmission to foremost universities. Held-back employees were pushed to the fore. Banned applicants were welcomed into exclusive societies and clubs. "Hopeless" failures were hauled up into success by successful rivals. People in trouble were saved by those who could help them. Obnoxious persons were welcomed by the cream of society. Unqualified aspirants were elevated into prized positions. Worthless men won stunning rich beauties. Bypassed women captured admired men. Inadequate employees were kept on payrolls. Fortune-making investment possibilities (like highly-valued properties up for distress sales) were thrown into the laps of the "lucky" ones for a mere "song." Housewives with moderate spending money have been directed to incredible bargains in furniture and other much-wanted goods. There is no end to the examples. Master the secret mental power to enthrall friend or enemy and turn the seemingly unavoidable failures in your life into roaring successes.

The Magic Difference in Your Life Resulting from Your Enthralling Even a Few Enemies

A philosopher once said that you could count your friends on the fingers of one hand, but your enemies on all the fingers of your hands, plus the toes of your feet. Your enemies, to be brief, outnumber your friends, perhaps far beyond what that philosopher said. Recently, a delirious man stood on the window ledge of a high story of a skyscraper and prepared to plunge to his death. A crowd quickly gathered below. When the man hesitated, the mob yelled, "Stop being chicken! Jump off!"

If anyone down there begged him not to, he was drowned out. That was by how many his enemies outnumbered his friends. Day after day you pass thousands of people on the streets who would egg you on similarly if you tried to commit suicide that way. Even some individuals whom you know for years might join them.

But don't let that turn you into a person who mistrusts or hates everybody. Just realize that if you can enthrall your *enemies* as well as your friends, you will *multiply* the number of people you can enthrall. That's why a politician with little chance to win can surge into office. His "enemies" are ready to vote against him, and if these constitute a sizable proportion of the total vote, they can trounce him. But if he can *add* them to his own support, even if they amount to but a small fraction of the total vote, he can win the election. Because once they vote for him they are *subtracted* from the opposition, thus *doubling* the effects of their numbers on the final count.

The same applies when you are being judged by a jury, or are hoping to be selected for a wanted post by an official board, waiting for an important offer, or praying to win a stupendous contract for yourself or your company, and the like. The little difference resulting from converting some of your enemies into boosters can catapult you to your goal *with little further effort on your part!*

How to Prevent Anybody, Anywhere, from Disliking You at Sight

The reasons why many people may dislike you at sight would fill thick volumes. It might emanate from a painful childhood experience of theirs with someone who happened to walk, talk, or peer at them like you; or from their acquired prejudices against someone with your complexion, hair color, nationality, race, religion, occupation, accent (even if from different regions of the same country), your possessions or lack of them, your age, your vocabulary or lack of it, your "air," the intensity of your glance, your mate, children, appetite, physical stature, education or lack of enough of it, political beliefs, life philosophies, and countless other reasons and combinations of each.

Since it is impossible to discover all the reasons or combinations of reasons why many people may dislike you at sight, you can't expect to prove to all such people that they may be wrong about you. But they do anger you and bristle your fight-sympathetics, and you fume secretly. That upsets your normal physiological language.

Their physiological languages, however, are also upset by the sight of you. So, both of you are suddenly dominated by your fight-sympathetics, and your heartbeats and your breathing are speeded up, and your muscles are hypertoned.

That, though, reveals how you *can prevent* people from disliking you at sight. You just have to normalize *their* physiological languages, and their dislikes for you vanish. Their dislikes for you (or for anything at all) cannot be nurtured without a fight-sympathetics' dominance of their physiological languages. It is similar to when someone is said to be in the "right mood" for something. It means that his body, triggered by his mind, is speaking the right physiological language to accept that "something." When his body is *not* speaking that right physiological language, it means that his mind has not triggered it and, consequently, he is not in the "right mood" to accept that something. When you *normalize* the physiological languages of people who dislike you at sight, then, their dislikes for you *vanish in an instant.* You thereby *prevent* them from disliking you at sight. Master that secret now with the physiological normal.

The Physiological Normalizing of Other People for Your Benefit

To normalize other people's physiological languages and thereby prevent them from disliking you at sight, normalize *your own* physiological language first. Your "air" or personality changes then without your even realizing it, and it shows in your eyes, your general attitude, your expression, your movements, and your speech. The persons you meet observe and "sense" that, and alter their impression of you.

To normalize your own physiological language, which has been upset since you spied a certain person, reflect to yourself that you *like* him tremendously (even if you actually dislike him). Imagine him to be *the ideal companion* for you, and behave toward him accordingly. When you gaze at him don't see *him* anymore, but imagine that you see that *ideal companion* instead! Your "air" or personality will change without your even being aware of it, and everyone will notice it and be instantly affected by it. He will either like you at once, or be soon doing so.

After you prevent him from disliking you, though, your next obstacle to controlling him swiftly, *after* you associate with him, is his inclination to see you as being ordinary. Learn how to clear this big hurdle with the physiological reversal.

The Physiological Reversal to Stop People from Considering You as Being Ordinary

Unless you possess an impressive appearance, a unique reputation, hold a degree from an Ivy League college, or a position of prominence in a highly-respected field, most people will be inclined to consider you as being ordinary, with no special appeal. Most people are impressed greatest by individuals they hear about but seldom, if ever, see. Once they observe them in the flesh and perceive that they are human beings with, perhaps, some commonplace freckles, some dental work, some typical posture faults, bulgy waistlines, or even wear glasses, the mystery about them disappears and they are regarded thenceforth as everyday people. It takes a dazzling personality, startling honesty, thrilling speech, exciting wit, or irresistible power of leadership, for the previously worshipped to regain their lost influence over that crowd. Hence, you cannot expect to meet and associate with people for long without their losing their awe of you and considering you as being ordinary.

How to Be Above Being Considered Merely Ordinary

This is how to prevent people from considering you as being ordinary, no matter how long you associate with them.

When people consider you as being ordinary, their physiological languages speak disinterestedly in regard to you. Their heartbeats and their breathing slow down from the abnormal speeds of a dominated fight-sympathetics to the lethargic pace of a bored, despising, half-drowsing parasympathetics dominance with a sympathetics slant. Even their muscles lose their hypertonicity and relax to a wishy-washy state. To stop them from considering you as being ordinary once they know you, *you have to stimulate their physiological languages to speak excitedly*! You have to quicken their heartbeats and their breathing into a state of zeal, and tone up their muscles into eager springs.

To do so, *forget yourself completely* and *think only of the other person.* See *him* as being something extraordinary, no matter if he is not. *Forcibly adopt a passion to help him in every possible way.* Don't fawn before him and behave like a nobody, but act as if you were ready to save the life of a kind-hearted but destitute friend. Flood your mind with that thought and forget your own sense of importance, and surge with enthusiasm for him. Your heart and breathing will spurt, and your muscles will pleasurably tense with gusto. You will feel contented and satisfied, and that will bring you a *sympathetics-parasympathetics balance.* With your body speaking this *right* physiological language, your eyes will pour out the look of unselfish love for mankind, and your lips will widen and your cheeks redden reflexively. (Your face will "brighten," as the novelists express it.)

This person, in turn, feels important because *you* treat him so flatteringly, and his body will speak the physiological language of satisfaction. His sympathetics and parasympathetics, in other words, will also balance each other. Your physiological languages now speak the same tongue. That's the secret of the physiological reversal. You have reversed the person you've worked upon from a bored, despising, half-drowsy parasympathetics dominance with a sympathetics slant, to a sympathetics-parasympathetics balance in your favor.

Why It Is Difficult to Understand Other People Quickly

To really understand other people quickly is far from easy. You might associate with them for years and think you know them through and through, only to be shocked by their unexpected future behavior. The situation is far worse when you are but superficially acquainted with the people. Yet you can't spend your life trying to understand others, for you meet too many individuals only socially and in business. The less time you associate with them, though, the faster you have to understand them or you will gain little from the contact with them. Clerks, policemen, receptionists, and salesmen face this problem continually. But even if you are, say, a teacher or a "boss," you still have to handle so many different persons regularly that you can hardly expect to understand them all individually. Still, you accomplish little with them unless you do. But you have too little time to understand the different physiological languages which their different minds and bodies speak toward you, and therefore you can't alter your own effectively enough to change theirs into the right physiological languages for you to enthrall.

But that difficulty vanishes when you use the secret mental power to enthrall friend or enemy. With it you can alter *anybody's* physiological language into speaking the right one for you to enthrall. You will learn how to master that secret power, as follows below.

How Make Everybody Like You and Want to Know You by Using the Right Physiological Language

When you meet a friend or an enemy, *banish completely from your mind any thought that he is either one or the other.* To a shrewd politician *everybody* is a potential voter! If the person votes for him, it is a friendly vote. If the person does not, it is a vote lost. To win the election the politician has to induce many unfriendly voters to vote for him, because he seldom can pull enough of his own followers' votes alone to put him in office. So he views everybody as a potential "friend" and shuts his mind to the fact that he also has "enemies" or enemy votes. When he loses a voter he does not view that person as an enemy, but as a potential vote lost! In his own mind, for that reason, he has no friends or enemies, but just votes gained for him, and votes not gained for him. Consequently, he campaigns to capture the votes he has not gained! With such an attitude he never looks upon the voters as consisting of friends and enemies of his, but as consisting of friends he has won, and of potential friends he is out to win!

That's precisely the attitude which you yourself have to adopt to enthrall your friends or enemies. Your mind then stops differentiating people between those who like you and those who dislike you, or between your friends and your enemies. You accept them all, rather, as friends you have won, and friends you have not yet won! Your physiological language then stops balancing itself when you meet a friend, and unbalancing itself when you meet an enemy.

How to Avoid Unnecessary Losses

Many bitter enmities, besides, are based on ludicrous misunderstandings. A friend or acquaintance of yours might happen to stare directly at you from across the street and fail to acknowledge your greeting merely because, for one reason or another, he didn't recognize you at the time. You despise him thereafter, for you now consider him rude, arrogant, or changeable. Or you might request a loan from him at a time when he is perilously obligated and is forced to refuse you. Or his romantic interest might throw a teasing glance at a platonic acquaintance of long standing and you instantly suspect a liaison.

To avoid losing a wanted associate through such a microscopic error, you should *view,* like the shrewd politician, *everybody as a potential friend.* You don't have to let yourself be victimized by others, nor should you keep company with individuals who lack character and are out to take advantage of you. But such extremes are rather obvious and count among the minority. It is with the great, perplexing majority that you have to use care.

A Simple Program for Mastery of Your Enemies

Sit alone in your room and think of your enemies. Train the physiological langauge of hate and fury that explodes within you then to calm down and alter into one of pleasurable appetite for something you madly crave to eat. Accomplish that by visualizing a most delicious dish *at the same time you think of your enemies.*

Practice and master this until your body speaks the right physiological language to make you feel toward your enemies as you feel toward your friends. When you can bring this change in you swiftly (and that will not take long), do it whenever you meet every "enemy." His attitude toward you will change instantly, despite himself, and he will find himself *liking you against his will*!

How to Trigger the Secret Mental Power to Enthrall Friend or Enemy with the Miracle Mind Magic Stimulator

Use the Miracle Mind Magic Stimulator to trigger the secret mental power to enthrall friend or enemy, and even to win back those whom you have alienated. Following is the secret to practice and master it.

Sit alone in your room and visualize yourself holding spellbound *everybody* you meet. Even "see" your worst enemy gazing back at you, ready to do anything for you. *That* is your goal, dream, or wish. Hold that vision in your mind for five seconds.

Then visualize that goal as coming true; visualize yourself facing *everybody* you meet, with the "right" expression on your face, saying the right things to them, treating them with flattering respect without demeaning yourself, advising them intelligently, praising them constructively, and entertaining them with your wit. Visualize yourself doing all of that like a totally spellbinding person. (If you have any trouble doing these things, consult Frank R. Young's *The Laws of Mental Domination*, Parker Publishing Co., West Nyack, N. Y.) Maintain that vision for four seconds.

Repeat that procedure three times, as you learned from practicing the Miracle Mind Magic Stimulator in Lesson 3. Intensify it each time and actually feel yourself change into *the very person* who can achieve that goal, dream, or wish to the utmost perfection. Feel every cell in your body change, so that you actually *become* such a person. Practice getting this feeling of *becoming him* until your nerves and muscles relax with the peace and contentment of total irresistibility. Practice it until you need to visualize this change just once, and to maintain it only two seconds, for your physiological language to speak like that of such a person. You will then be ready to trigger the secret mental power to enthrall friend or enemy and easily prevent people from disliking you at sight, from seeing you as being ordinary, as well as to make everybody like you and want to know you.

Below are case histories of people who used the secret mental power to enthrall friends or enemies for profit every day of their lives. Their names have been changed. Study them well and do still better yourself.

How Esther F. Ended the Suicidal Tendency
of Her Hard-Pressed College Student Son

Esther F. worried desperately over her youngest son, Art. Her husband demanded that he score all A's in college. Art was a conscientious student, but he pleaded that he had no "camera mind," that he couldn't excel in the predominantly memorizing subjects, no matter how hard he strained. It was a pity, he grieved, that so many of his major subjects were of that type. Many a graduate school, his father warned him, would deny him a degree unless he maintained a B average. It wasn't his fault, Art replied in frustration, if the colleges didn't teach their subjects more creatively. "You can't change everything you disagree with in life!" his father snapped back. "You have to face many problems as they are *and do better with them than the other fellow!* You'll waste your whole life just struggling and getting nowhere otherwise!"

Esther watched her frantic son, her heart beating wildly. Parental pressure to make good grades, she had read, was helping drive the suicide rate among college students to an all-time high. Esther dreaded that Art might do something drastic to himself once he returned to class after the holidays, so many hundreds of miles away. (All the kids, it seemed, wanted to attend schools far from home, she thought.) Since going to college, she noted, Art had already acquired a disheveled appearance and a worried, harried, furrowed brow. He confessed to Esther in private that, due to all the pressure on him, he now had difficulty concentrating; that the printed word no longer carried meaning to him; that he brooded and daydreamed and sat all day, at times, listening to hi-fi music.

Esther was afraid to take him to a psychiatrist, so I taught her the secret mental power to enthrall friend or enemy. Art, after all, viewed her now as a foe because she, too, had to press him to raise his grades or be left without a career. She therefore realized that he had come to dislike her at sight.

With the Miracle Mind Magic Stimulator Esther triggered this secret mental power and normalized her terribly upset physiological language. Then she normalized Art's, too, with the physiological normal. She then persuaded him to do his best, assuring him that the future would take care of itself after that.

Art wept on her shoulder, as he had as a child. With his physiological language normalized he was tremendously relieved, and he studied once more with a relaxed frame of mind. His grades improved soon and, in the remaining years, he raised them more than high enough to qualify for his degree.

How Bill K. Saved Himself From a Long General Layoff

Keen competition was crushing the company which Bill K. had worked for ever since he grew up. To save it from disaster, it was rumored, big cost-cutting plans for it were in the making. One of them would hand dispensable employees long layoffs, amounting to permanent dismissal. Many older employees would be among them, to save on their bigger salaries and enlarging pensions. Being one of those, Bill was scared to death, particularly because Mr. Andrews, a semiretired founder of the plant, wielded strong clout in it. Bill had unnecessarily defied him several years ago when Mr. Andrews had been fully active on the premises and had made an enemy of him.

A man in his mid-fifties could not find a new position easily, Bill told me, pouring out his terrors to me. I taught him the secret mental power to enthrall friend or enemy. Bill couldn't concentrate enough to master it, so worried was he; but when someone hinted to him, from the grapevine, that he *would* be laid off at the end of the month, Bill mastered the secret mental power overnight. He triggered it the next day with the Miracle Mind Magic Stimulator and normalized his frenzied physiological language. Through some ruse he made his way into Mr. Andrews' office and applied the physiological reversal on him. Mr. Andrews' whole attitude toward him changed. At the end of the month, a long list of older employees were laid off–but not Bill. A year later Bill was still with the company, and Mr. Andrews had retired altogether and had recommended him for a desirable promotion.

SUMMARY OF THIS SECRET MENTAL POWER

To enthrall friend or enemy is to multiply the number of people you influence in life because, like everybody else, you usually have far more enemies than friends. According to the old saying, "A friend in need is a friend indeed." (Many a seeming friend does not prove to be so friendly when you need him.) But you *can* convert your potential enemies (as well as your active enemies) into friends and thereby multiply the number of people in life whom you influence. Otherwise you influence too few and your path through life, socially or in business, degenerates into a hard, maddening one. With this secret mental power you soon have *even your enemies* eating out of your hand. To acquire it, follow these simple routines:

1. Whenever you encounter a friend or an enemy, reassure yourself that *everybody* is a potential friend.
2. Prevent others from disliking you at sight with the physiological normal.
3. Then prevent them from seeing you as being ordinary, with the physiological reversal.
4. With the Miracle Mind Magic Stimulator, trigger regularly the right physiological language to enthrall friend or enemy even before you meet them, and become *the very person* who can enthrall them.

Lesson 12

Your Secret Mental Power
for Most Effective Judgment

Sensible judgment provides you with the magic ability to "pick the right way" to realize any goal, dream, or wish. It leads you past devastating experiences like those that held you back in the past and which can hold you back in the future. It selects for you the best way, the easiest way, the shortest road to attain your ideals. Your every move in life becomes economical and effective, for it reduces the need for chance-taking. It even by-passes the advantages of study and knowledge alone. Some call it "instinct" and "sixth sense" and explain it as a psychic gift, but it is actually a swift solving of anything baffling by your conscious mind, with the help of your computerlike subconscious mind. But it stuns others with your acuity, and they assume that you possess some unearthly gift.

Actually, all puzzling situations disturb your physiological language, and that befogs your mind and prevents you from thinking clearly. With the secret mental power for most sensible judgment, you normalize your physiological language and use your hidden powers of thinking to the full! You then possess the magic ability to pick the right way to realize any goal, dream, or wish.

The Fantastic Profits from Most Sensible Judgment

The profits certain people have enjoyed from most sensible judgment baffle the best computer. With it they met crises which

141

drove others to despair, or even to suicide, and not only overcame them, but skyrocketed to the top out of the ruins. Some rose out of utter devastation to become multimillionaires. Others practically crawled out of the grave to burst with health. Persons who were being victimized by the selfish, freed themselves from their shackles and lived joyful lives. Many, whose big opportunities were imperiled by emotional factors, controlled these and realized their lifetime dreams. Many who took unnecessarily bold risks became intelligently cautious and achieved their goals much easier and faster. Others who were enslaved by greed constrained themselves and amassed riches without even "trying." Individuals who contemplated revolutionary changes in their lives changed their minds and attained their goals by staying right where they were and by doing what they had always done. Others, faced with staggering troubles, solved these to their utmost satisfaction and astronomical profit. The list is endless of how people changed their whole lives in an instant with the secret mental power for most sensible judgment.

The Nine Main Causes That Hinder You from Arriving at the Most Sensible Judgment in Your Everyday Life

There are nine main causes that hinder you repeatedly from arriving at most sensible judgment in your everyday life. These are:

1. Your self-defeating blind stubbornness against accepting cold facts, or the advice of others which disagrees with your own.
2. Your indomitable insistence on always having your own way.
3. Your tenacious clinging to old comfortable routines.
4. Your fierce resentment of criticism.
5. Your explosive impatience to learn new procedures or techniques "instantly."
6. Your fear of failure in taking new steps or performing new routines.
7. Your feeling of having lost your importance with the discarded old steps or old routines.

8. Your blind impulse to change your residence or your career unnecessarily.

9. Your tendency to be blinded by the superficial attraction of greener fields.

You will be taught how to overcome any of these nine causes whenever they induce you to form disastrous judgment.

1. How to Overcome Your Self-Defeating Blind Stubbornness

Every situation that arouses blind stubbornness in you routs your normal physiological language and robs you of the confidence, superiority, and importance which you enjoyed with your "old self," and leaves you under the dominance of your dread-sympathetics. This condition resembles the initial symptoms of faintness. Your heart beats fast as your sympathetics try to rescue you from the dread. But the dread takes the power out of your heartbeat. The blood pours into your muscles to fight the dread, leaving so little for your brain to think clearly that you feel giddy and break into the cold sweat of terror at your all-over debility. Your blood pressure falls because comparatively little blood remains in your arteries, you turn pale, and your hands and feet grow cold from lack of normal circulation. So you feel faint and defenseless.

To normalize this resulting panicky physiological language, fold your hands tightly together for one second to let your dread-sympathetics discharge the energy of their terror from your right hand to your left hand (or vice versa, if you are left-handed). That rids you of your terror, but still retains their nerve energy within your body.

Immediately afterward, *forget yourself completely* and stare unemotionally at the cold facts that triggered your blind stubbornness, or listen closely to the opinions of others which disagree with yours about the situation. *Compel* yourself to feel that you are about to profit *tremendously* by doing so. *Accept the fact* that the evidence of the cold facts or of the opinions of others who are trying to help you *may be truly worthwhile*, and that they may help you circumvent disaster and leap ahead of the obstacle you face. And that once you leap ahead of it, you can be yourself again and continue with your previous plans or actions, and keep them running smoothly now. *Expect* to change your plans, to meet the trying situation effectively, but realize that you will be the gainer for it. Your heartbeat will slow down and regain its normal power, and you will feel confident, like your "old self" again.

2. How to Control the Tendency to Always Have Your Own Way

When you insist on having your own way (usually due to your protective ego, or because you don't respect the counsel of others), your normal physiological langauge becomes dominated by your fight-sympathetics. Your heart pounds hard and strong, and your muscles become firm. But you feel as if you are walking on a precipice because you have no positive assurance that your own way is the right way. Back in your mind is the fear that your methods have been bringing in failure of late, and that you and your associates are trying to figure out what is wrong. A dread-sympathetics tendency, for that reason, tries to dominate your physiological language next and combats the symptoms of the fight-sympathetics which already dominate it. And so, your heart pounds hard, fast, and strong one moment, then speedily but weakly the next (clinically called "thready pulse"). This to-and-fro alteration practically prostrates you. Your physiological language is speaking a dual tongue of savage rage and weak-kneed anxiety.

To normalize this freakish physiological language, fold your hands tightly together for one second to let your dread-sympathetics and your fight-sympathetics discharge the energy of their combatting fury from your right hand to your left hand (or vice versa, if you are left-handed). That pacifies them, but still retains their energy within your body.

Immediately afterward, analyze with a cool, open mind the methods of others. Don't just subdue your own ego, but *put to the test the methods of others*—and *compel* yourself to do it with *as much enthusiasm* as if they were *your own.* Temporarily become *those other persons*, in other words, so you speak their normal physiological languages and control your ruinous tendency of always wanting your own way. You will swiftly possess sensible judgment.

3. How to Stop Clinging Tenaciously to Old Routines

It is only natural to grow accustomed to an old routine and feel at home in it, because you enjoy doing whatever you do well. Your body responds by speaking a physiological language of perfectly balanced sympathetics-parasympathetics nervous systems control. Your heart and breathing speeds are then normal; your muscles are filled with normal, flexible muscle tone; and your brain with normal blood flow, to think and act sanely and efficiently. But when suddenly faced with the necessity of adopting a new routine to which you are a stranger, you are "thrown off" your stride and feel lost. The shock upsets your perfectly balanced physiological language, and you fall into the extinguishing grip of your dread-sympathetics. You feel helpless— even nauseated—and acquire a heated hatred of the new routine, and cling tenaciously to the old one.

To normalize this upset physiological language, fold your hands tightly together for one second to let your fear-sympathetics discharge the energy of their terror from your right hand to your left hand (or vice versa, if you are left-handed). That balances them again, but retains the nerve energy of their upheaval within your body.

Immediately afterward, throw yourself into the new routine *as if you had never known the old one.* Come to the new one with the eyes of a newborn babe who is doing something exciting for the first time, not with a feeling of anger and regret for having to change something you had grown accustomed to and enjoyed doing. Every time anything reminds you of the old routine, stamp it out of your mind, like something dead and forgotten, or which never existed. That will keep your physiological language normalized and adapt you to the new routine.

4. How to Stop Resenting Criticism

Criticism chops you in two as a person, especially when it is directed at something in which you consider yourself excellent. It crucifies you, in addition, when you are trying to master something new and make laughable mistakes. It confuses you because you are struggling to do your best. To be told then that you are still doing it wrong makes you feel that you can *never* do it right; that you are wasting your time (and perhaps money, too), attempting the impossible. Worse still, you might be thrilled by your own efforts and feel that you are performing expertly.

To be told then that your achievement is amateurish throws you into a frenzy. You rage at your critic, and that inflames your fight-sympathetics. Your heart beats faster, your breathing quickens, and your arteries overtense. Your muscles overtone, and your brain turns savage. You are unable to proceed smoothly with your efforts, for the criticism leaves you tight with tension. So you give way to the fear of making still more mistakes, and that, in turn, stimulates your fear-sympathetics. Your mind and body then speak the unbalanced physiological language of the desperate person—the tongue of savage rage alternating with weak-kneed anxiety; of muscles possessing Herculean power one moment, but altering to paralytic the next; and of a brain turning from furious thinking one moment, to near-hysteria the next. In such a state, most sensible judgment is impossible.

To normalize this tempestuous physiological language, fold your hands tightly together for one second to let your inflamed fight-sympathetics and your frenzied fear-sympathetics discharge the combined energy of their criticism-hating from your right hand to your left hand (or vice-versa, if you are left-handed). That rids you of their storming, but retains their nerve energy within your body.

Immediately afterward, *expect* the criticism and *enjoy* receiving it. Accept it as being *the very instruction you need* to perfect your efforts. Instead of wasting time resenting it, spend that time trying to interpret it as accurately as possible and in figuring out how to apply it best. Expect to fail, too, when you apply it; but instead of turning bitter, study it still more closely and apply it again. Realize, also, that as soon as you apply it right, you will be closer than before to perfecting your skill. You will then be *ahead* of him who is not receiving and using that criticism. (It is taken for granted that your critic is intelligent, informed, and well-meaning.) Your physiological language will then normalize itself again, and you will stop resenting the criticism and gain fully from it.

5. How to Control Your Explosive Impatience to Learn New Procedures or Techniques "Instantly"

You will always be impatient when you try to learn a new procedure or technique, particularly when it requires you to unlearn an old one. The child learns easier than the adult because it has little to unlearn. You may have to learn just so much of the new thing at a time, too, and to retrace your steps to master certain details before you can proceed further. (That applies even to learning a hobby.) Consequently, you rage at yourself for taking so long to master the new technique. That alters your normal physiological language: first, into a fear-sympathetics, as you note that you are not absorbing the new procedure or routine as rapidly as you wish; and then into a fight-sympathetics, as you rage at the fact that you can't master it as swiftly as you'd hoped to. Your heartbeat, your muscle tone, and your mental calm rip loose as a result, rendering most sensible judgment impossible.

To normalize this savage physiological language and keep cool, fold your hands tightly together for one second to let your fear- and fight-sympathetics discharge their explosive energy from your right hand to your left hand (or vice versa, if you are left-handed). That rids you of their civil war, but retains their nerve energy within your body.

Immediately afterward, realize that you are not going to learn the new procedure or routine at once. To learn anything requires a certain period of time. The mile-runner realizes that he can't cover the distance in ten seconds, no matter how fast he sprints. He needs closer to four minutes. But he must maintain a winning pace from start to finish. Even after running for two minutes, he still has another two or so to go. Meanwhile, he must keep running quickly but calmly and not worry himself to get there "at once," or he'll exhaust himself in no time. He must do so even at the three and a half minute mark. The athlete could not perform it, either, at some time in the past. Like him, you too have to go along calmly practicing it, until you master it. Your normalized physiological language will then control your impatience, and you will use your most sensible judgment to learn the new procedure or technique.

6. How to Lose Your Fear of Failure in
Taking New Steps or Performing New Routines

Your fear of failure in taking new steps or performing a new routine will seize you repeatedly before your performance is expert. Each time you fail before you master it is a catastrophe to you, because it leaves you doubting whether you will ever learn it. You make the least mistakes when you are calm, cool, and collected, because your muscles are then most flexible and relaxed. Fear of failure, though, winds you up like a clock and paralyzes you with tension whenever you take the least action. Your fear-sympathetics seize you and overtense your muscles, and your physiological language breaks loose in frustration and you make more mistakes than ever.

To normalize your frustrated physiological language and lose that resulting fear of failure, fold your hands tightly together for one second to let your fear-sympathetics discharge their overtoning energy from your right hand to your left hand (and vice versa, if you are left-handed). That rids you of their muscle overtensing, but retains their nerve energy within your body.

Immediately afterward, think with amusement at your fear of failure. Consider it as just one more step on your way to mastering the new routine—just one less step to make. Don't estimate how many similar failures you may have to suffer before mastering it, either. Just call each one *one failure less* to suffer, and continue with the practice or performance and try to avoid repeating the cause of the last failure. But should you repeat it, consider that, too, as just another failure less to suffer, for some causes of failures may be harder for one person to overcome than another. Your physiological language will then be freed of the frustration, and you will continue taking the new step or practicing the new routine with the same ease that you did the old routine. Your fear of failure in performing it will vanish, and you will use most sensible judgment to learn it fast.

7. How to Nullify Your Feeling of Having
Lost Your Importance with the Discarded
Old Steps or Old Routines

Your feeling of having lost your importance in a discarded old routine will prevent you from focusing your full attention upon the new one and mastering it. You will be as distracted, as if suffering from nostalgia after leaving a wonderful place to move about in a totally strange and confusing one. You still will subconsciously retain the old skill, however, and your muscles will resist adapting to the new one. Your fear-sympathetics will dominate your physiological language, and your mind will be too distraught to use most sensible judgment and master the new routine.

To normalize your distraught-creating physiological language, fold your hands tightly together for one second to let your fear-sympathetics discharge their embarrassing energy from your right hand to your left hand (or vice versa, if you are left-handed). That rids you of their annihilation, but retains their nerve energy within your body.

Immediately afterward, realize that your importance will now rest with your mastery of the *new* routine. So, the sooner you master the new routine, without rushing, the sooner you will be important again. Stop thinking about regaining your importance or superiority, though, for that keeps reminding you of the status you lost with the *discarded* technique. Think alone of the *new* technique and all it offers you once you master it—which you can expect before long. Your physiological language will then accept the new routine as *the thing* to react to. Your conscious mind will nullify your feeling of having lost your status with the discarded routine and, with most sensible judgment, you will master the new one in a surprisingly short time.

8. How to Banish a Senseless Impulse to Change Your Residence or Your Career

The despair of mastering a new procedure or technique fast enough can upset you and drive you to seek a new career altogether. (This applies equally to adjusting yourself socially or to anything else.) It always seems easier to fly into something new than to try to save the old. This is true not only of careers but of domestic life as well, and accounts for much of the staggering divorce rate. Your fight-sympathetics then dominate your physiological language, your muscles overtense, and you abandon your career, your marriage, your friendships, your business, or whatever else presents you with a seemingly unsolvable problem.

To normalize your recklessly-inciting physiological language, fold your hands tightly together for one second to let your fight-sympathetics discharge their super muscle-tensing energy from your right hand to your left hand (or vice versa, if you are left-handed). That rids you of their restless drive, but retains their nerve energy within your body.

Immediately afterward convince yourself that your situation or occupation is *the* one—the *only one*—the *best one* for you. *That* is the one you have to make good in, tell yourself, for you are already in it and are familiar with it. You just have to keep adjusting to the trifling new changes in it, and you will be as satisfied as you were before. What does it matter if you don't learn its new procedures at once and easily? Another situation or career might be even more difficult for you to learn or accept! Your normalized physiological language will then stop recklessly inciting you, and you will relax and analyze your difficulties with most sensible judgment before making an impatient move which you may regret later.

9. How Not to Be Blinded by the Superficial Attractions of Greener Fields

Newspaper articles, advertisements, and fidgety people who are impossible to satisfy, constantly impel you to change your field of work or your habitat and to venture into others, which they describe as being far more glamorous, exciting, pleasant, and even more lucrative. Such unproved effusions depress you, dissatisfy you with your present life, and lower your efficiency in your career or social life.

As a consequence, they alter your normal physiological language into an angry-sympathetics. You start detesting your friends, your environment, and your job, and live in a dream world. This mental poison grows until you are more dissatisfied with your lot than a true unfortunate who is without work, funds, friends, or future, and who loathes everybody and everything wherever he lives. You develop into an unendurable grouch and either weary others with your complaints or turn into a butt for their jibes, and get worse and worse. You can no longer form sensible judgments about your present situation or occupation and turn into another Don Quixote, pursuing the impossible dream, ready to throw everything over and burst out wildly into a nonexistent world of fantasy.

To normalize this mentally poisoning physiological language, fold your hands tightly together for one second to let your angry-sympathetics discharge their hate-filled energy from your right hand to your left hand (and vice versa, if you are left-handed). That rids you of their wrathful indignation, but retains their nerve energy within your body.

Immediately afterward, realize that the utopias you read or hear about can't last long, even if they do exist. Once a "little," sparsely-settled locale is heralded widely as being "one of the last remaining uncrowded, unspoiled spots left on earth," legions of visitors flock to it and it can't remain uncrowded and unspoiled for long. The same applies to careers, or anything else. (Look at the surplus supply of science Ph.D.'s, teachers, etc., that resulted from similar advice.) Accept that obvious, realistic fact and stop deluding yourself, and use your most sensible judgment before making any important move.

How to Trigger Your Most Sensible Judgment with the Miracle Mind Magic Stimulator

To trigger this secret mental power the moment you face anything that dissatisfies you, and which converts you into a physiological language wreck and blinds you to applying your most sensible judgment to it, use the Miracle Mind Magic Stimulator. It will normalize your wrecking physiological language into that of the person who would use most sensible judgment to prevent him from being victimized. So, practice and master the Miracle Mind Magic Stimulator for this secret mental power.

Your Personal Program

Sit alone in your room and visualize your dissatisfied self changing into a self who would be *totally satisfied* with your present life. Ignore the fact that there is a lot to be dissatisfied about. Your objective with the Miracle Mind Magic Stimulator is to keep the reins on yourself, so you will always use most sensible judgment in everything you do. That is your goal, dream, or wish. Hold that picture of your changed self for five seconds.

Then visualize that goal as coming true; visualize yourself changing completely and thinking as you *would* think if you were suddenly changed into such a thoroughly satisfied self. Maintain that vision for four seconds.

Repeat that procedure three times, as you learned from practicing the Miracle Mind Magic Stimulator in Lesson 3. Intensify it each time, so you actually *feel yourself change* into that kind of self. Practice bringing on this sensation until you glow with the satisfaction that your present life is a true utopia (no matter if that is farthest from the truth). Practice this until you can convert yourself into such a self with one visualization, lasting only two seconds. Your physiological language will then speak like that of such a self, and you will be able to trigger the secret mental power for most sensible judgment instantly thereafter and spare yourself the resulting catastrophe of making, and following, ruinous decisions.

Below are case histories of people who used this secret mental power for everyday profit. Their names have been changed. Study them and profit from it even more than they have.

How Joe T. Saved His Work Energy Daily by Doing Far More Work with Far Less Effort

Joe T.'s occupation required speed and precision. It required speed to maintain a high enough output, and precision to turn out workable products to render satisfactory service. Unless he kept up with those "musts," Joe would be *out*, and he knew it. With them, though, he provided well for his family and was building up enviable independence. But they were wearing him out, and he was in his fifties. His vacations no longer restored him as they once did. Younger men and more advanced equipment brought him keener competition. To remain in the swim, Joe had to work still faster, and with more precision! But there was a limit to his time and energy.

He confessed his appalling problem to me. Realizing how badly upset his physiological language was, I taught him the secret mental power of sensible judgment, and the nine causes that hindered him from solving his problem.

Joe mastered the secret mental power in short order and listed the main causes which hindered him from arriving at the most sensible judgment about his dilemma. He overcame them one by one, and concluded that he had to do far more work with far less effort.

At work the next day, Joe triggered the right physiological language for most sensible judgment with the Miracle Mind Magic Stimulator. He soon discovered that, although he worked at a slower pace with that physiological language, *he completed more work!* He studied his movements closely to find out why. He did more work then, he saw, because, when his physiological language was normal, he was calm, cool, steady of hand, made less mistakes, wasted less moves, and tired less! *That increased his precision!* To increase his output he just had to work *with more rhythm.* The rhythm made his movements practically effortless and automatic, and increased his speed *without his working as fast.* With his normalized physiological language, his muscle action synchronized with his heartbeat and breathing without his even realizing it, and linked up with them in a physiological waltz. Joe was promptly doing far more work with far less effort.

How Larry N. Raised His I.Q. Into That of an
Executive Genius in Seconds

Larry N. was sick and tired of being held back from reaching the top in his department because his superiors did not consider him "practical enough." His I.Q. was satisfactory, but his superiors felt that he was swayed too easily by emotion, by pity, by philanthropy, by unbusinesslike soft-heartedness, by impetuosity to please everybody, by excess pride and supersensitivity, and even by a tendency to take unnecessary chances, all of which were dangerous qualities for anyone in a position overseeing large sums of company money.

They accepted Larry as being honest to an angelic degree, but feared that he might be a babe in arms when dealing with the unscrupulous and end up in jail, as well as leave the firm in an embarrassing position. Larry admitted to me that he was probably generous to a fault, and at times blindly so. Yet, by denying him the promotion he was entitled to, his firm also denied him top pay, top pension, top prestige, and the position he deserved.

Aware of his resulting tumultuous physiological language, I taught him the secret mental power for most sensible judgment.

Larry studied carefully the main causes that hindered him from arriving at the most sensible ("practical") judgment at work. That normalized his physiological language, and he perceived which causes cursed him with the unbusinesslike qualities which had barred him from reaching new heights. Every time one of them dominated him, he discovered, his physiological language burst into a wild revelry and deprived him of level-headedness. He realized now that one could _not_ handle other people's money wisely with such ebullience. With a normalized physiological language, however, he became practical and handled the firm's business soundly with the secret mental power for most sensible judgment.

At work thereafter, Larry triggered that secret mental power with the Miracle Mind Magic Stimulator. His superiors noted that he made one remarkable practical move after another. They were so impressed with him that, by the end of the year, they promoted him to head of his department—to the position he aspired to.

SUMMARY OF THIS SECRET MENTAL POWER

By using most sensible judgment you can achieve _any_ possible goal, dream, or wish in life _even if you don't qualify for it_—because with it you automatically select _the best way_ to pursue it. No other mental power can surpass it. To acquire this truly magic miracle power, follow these simple routines:

1. When confronted with anything that requires a most careful decision, examine at once the nine main causes which may hinder you from arriving at the most sensible judgment for it.
2. Overcome each and every one of those nine main causes, particularly the ones that apply most to you.
3. With the Miracle Mind Magic Stimulator trigger the right physiological language into you for using the secret mental power of most sensible judgment.
4. Tackle the problem again, and you will be astonished at how easily the best way to solve it flashes through your mind.

This Page Intentionally Left Blank

Many with limited funds invested in the "right" businesses for future growth and became rich in a few years. Others changed the whole slant of their grown businesses the moment their profits stopped increasing, and made them skyrocket again. People in different callings studied, in their leisure hours, other branches of their occupation just before these came into big demand and reaped a staggering harvest. Individuals changed bad habits into healthy ones and altered the whole course of their lives. Cautious persons refused to be rushed into fashions on a business basis or to engage in big money-making activities which they feared might endanger their health, and lived to stay comparatively young and healthy, while the short-sighted, greedy ones paid for their folly unendingly. Others left attractive positions for others paying less, but moved to where they could live "as if in heaven." For any possible goal, dream or wish, the secret mental power for wisest future action will show you the easiest and surest way to achieve it, and guide you to it as if by magic. That's why it is, indeed, the miracle of mind magic. Master it by learning the eight secret, simple steps of the Success Dial. These are described below:

1. The Handicap of Envying Those Who Succeed Where You Fail

Nothing can prevent you more from planning your wisest future action in anything than to envy those who succeed where you fail. In addition to wasting your time, your clear thinking for future action is muddled and twisted by the gnawing recollection of "what a fool" you made of yourself, of "how lucky" the other person was, and of how unlucky you yourself were.

But that's not all. Once you form the habit of envying another person, you are not satisfied until you rip him to shreds analytically. If you envy him for succeeding in his career while you, yourself, were only mediocre in yours, you proceed to find fault with his appearance, his speech, his children, his home, his car, his friends and acquaintances, his golf, his table manners—in fact, with anything and everything about him. This mental habit alters your normal physiological language into a bitter fight-sympathetics and speeds up your heartbeat (or raises your blood pressure) and hypertones your muscles into chronic pugnacity.

Before long, this attitude dominates your whole personality, and people classify you as a "doom-or-gloom crab." You cannot make decisions for wisest future action then because you can hardly think straight. Your uncontrolled envy of others has wreaked havoc with your physiological language.

2. How to Boldly Review Your Past Mistakes

To make up for your past failures, boldly review your mistakes that caused them. This is a painful procedure because it compels you to blame yourself for them. "To succeed," you have repeated again and again to yourself, "one needs pull!" So, you have stopped detecting the opportunistic openings lying around the pull: openings which the alert take advantage of. You refuse to realize that "pull" has always existed, but that great numbers of people achieve their goals, dreams or wishes by squeezing through it. To do so, though, you have to plan your wisest future action, or you can never squeeze through the opening in the pull. But "pull" will never leave the earth, no matter what type of government or society rules. But with wisest future action you can grab ahold of the rope of "pull" yourself and let it pull *you* up for a change!

You can detect the openings in the "pull" by boldly reviewing your past mistakes. To detect them, cease pining over the injustices which you feel or know you have suffered from, and behold your past efforts with the eyes of *someone who would have succeeded* in your place, despite all. Do so with Success Dial 1 (page 162).

Behold, next, the past mistakes which *you, yourself*, made that caused you to fail in your efforts. You will then understand why the other person succeeded with the identical opportunities which *you* missed. Do so with Success Dial 2 (page 162).

Find out, next, what steps the successful person would *not* have taken—were he in your place. Those are the steps which *you* yourself took—and which led to your making the past mistakes that caused you to fail in your efforts. Do so with Success Dial 3 (page 163).

To use your personality to get "pull," remember, is no crime. To shun "pull" rudely but still expect to be favored, though, is more like a crime, for then you are expecting something for nothing.

3. How to Boldly Analyze How You Could Have Avoided Making Your Past Mistakes

Most mistakes in life (particularly, the serious ones) are usually due to minor oversights or misinterpretations. A whole building is burned down, for instance, merely because a tenant forgot to put out his cigarette. A valuable document is rendered worthless because it lacks a comma in one sentence, or because the signature lacks the middle initial, or because it bears a slightly wrong date. Both Napoleon and Hitler failed to conquer Russia only because the winters they invaded her turned out to be the coldest in decades. (Had they planned for such an eventuality ahead of time with wisest future action, they could have prepared for it with the same ingenuity they had used to conquer that vast country before the onset of winter.) A small precaution not taken, or an unexpected possibility overlooked, has ruined the most ingenious plans. That's how the best-thought-out crimes are usually solved. The cleverest criminals are caught through piddling oversights on their parts.

By boldly analyzing your past mistakes, you give yourself a thorough character analysis. You then know what your weaknesses are and can prevent them from hindering you in the future. That is a big step toward your planning wisest future action.

4. The Most Probable Result from any, "Move" You Make

Reviewing your past mistakes alone, though, won't enable you to plan your wisest future action. It will lead you away from making significant mistakes when taking similar action in the future, but it will not map for you the best road to follow in the future to attain your goal, dream or wish. To map the best road you have to list, first, what will probably result from any move you make in it. Don't wait until *after* making your moves (and your mistakes) to analyze them and figure out how you could have avoided making them. It is too late, then. It is better *to avoid making them in the first place.* Achieve that by anticipating *beforehand* as many of your potential mistakes as you can, and prepare to steer clear of them. Do so with Success Dial 4 (page 163).

Note: To carry out some of your plans might inconvenience you more than you expected. Or they might depend upon the reliability of others. Whenever the human factor is introduced into anything, be ready to be able to continue *alone* with your plans if you have to. Even the sickness or death of someone could alter your plans.

5. The Best Way to Proceed with Each Plan

Since you want the utmost gain from each plan, you should *shoot for the stars.* You underrate yourself, otherwise, and expect only the crumbs. Don't let others undermine your morale by terrifying you with suggested limitations. Free yourself from this crushing drawback with Success Dial 5 (page 164). With Success Dial 5 you forget about pitfalls and visualize yourself achieving your goal, dream or wish swiftly. You become a dreamer, but remain realistic enough. Ignore the fact that a million dollars is not easy to accumulate. If you yearn for a mate who seems outside of your reach, just scoff at the obstacles. If you aspire for promotion or an opportunity which seems unattainable, just cast out the doubts. If you pine for a classic figure or for a godly health, just crush out all discouragement. Whatever you plan for, feel and think that you *can* achieve it easily and swiftly.

6. The Worst Way to Proceed with Each Plan

But sometimes the best of plans don't work out. That's because you do not foresee the serious obstacles (big or small) that stand in your way. And so they catch you unprepared. You turn angry and impatient and your physiological language goes berserk. So, you do *the first thing that comes into your head*—and end up in disaster! If you only suspect beforehand *what* these obstacles are, you can prepare for them and sail right past them. *One* unexpected obstacle is usually the one that causes your downfall. To make sure you don't miss it, consider next, the *worst possible things* that could happen to you from the venture. Do it with Success Dial 6 (page 165).

7. How to Anticipate Your Money-Making Mistakes Beforehand—and Avoid Them

You can anticipate your future mistakes in any undertaking, whether it be business, social, health, or any other kind. You just have to be aware of one or more of the following pitfalls: Be aware of

1. The possible economic barriers in your way
2. The possible obstacles of the expected competition
3. The possible legal stumbling blocks
4. The dire possibilities of the changing times, such as the different fads, philosophies, interests, customs, environments, difficulty of procuring goods or materials
5. The time limits, both on yourself and on your chances of success
6. The unpredictable sudden needs for ready cash, not only for the venture, but for yourself or your family
7. The struggle against weather, distance, growing expenses and rising costs
8. The need for sufficient room
9. The need for safety, insurance and legal protection of the assets (equipment, trademarks, copyrights, etc.) to be acquired
10. Even the possibilities of your home changing, or breaking up because of it

The aim is to anticipate all possible eventualities. Then you can prepare yourself to meet any of the obstacles to your making big money. *You must no longer be caught by surprise, come what may*! You will know how to bail out safely in the midst of the most dangerous money-making scheme. Let Success Dials 7 and 8 (pages 166 and 167) perform that fantastic job for you.

8. Prepare as Thoroughly for the Best and the Worst

You are now like the observer staring down at a city from the top of a mountain or from an airplane. He perceives every road, and the traffic on each. The person driving a car on a road, in contrast, sees mainly the other cars on his road.

So, think now what you would do if the *best* happened to your undertaking. What would you do with all the money you made? What would you do if you got the big promotion or the big opportunity? If you expanded your venture, how would you do it? Would it require more money, more of your time, a partner or more partners? Would it force you to change locations? Require more education? More helpers? More sources of cheaper products or materials? Etc., etc.? Your answer is in Success Dial 9 (page 168).

But suppose the *worst* happened to your undertaking. Suppose you don't make enough money from it? Suppose you don't land the big promotion or the big opportunity? Suppose you have to file bankruptcy? What if your partner or partners disappointed you or lost interest? Suppose you have to change locations but lack the funds to do so? What if competition grows so keen that you have to quit (no matter if the undertaking is a social or business one)? Suppose you lack enough education to make a big go of your project? Suppose you are swamped with business, but can't make a decent profit if you take in help? Suppose your costs skyrocket, but you are charging all the market will bear? Suppose the mate you crave has already fallen for someone else? Etc., etc.? Your answer is in Success Dial 10 (page 169).

Let nothing about your undertaking, to repeat tiresomely, *catch you by surprise*! Be prepared for *any* eventuality in it by having considered it, or something like it, *beforehand.* You will then always retain the right physiological language for wisest future action.

Note: You will find going through the Success Dials as thrilling as writing your own autobiography *as you wish it had happened.* You will be using your past experiences to plot your future moves in life *like a true wizard.*

SUCCESS DIAL 1

THE SUCCESSFUL STEPS OF SOMEONE WHO WOULD HAVE SUCCEEDED WHERE I FAILED

1. Don't venture too deeply before I have enough experience. Don't depend upon "novice luck."
2. Check up thoroughly before making a move. (And be prepared to save myself if that move is wrong.)
3. If it is for commercial profit, be sure to have a *legal okay.*
4. I have enough funds to carry me through a bad beginning.
5. I will save funds to carry me through unexpected upsets.
6. I will do better without a partner. (Or, I am taking on a partner *without illusions* about his faults.)
7. I don't expect absolute perfection in my efforts, but I don't expect to give up at the first sign of failure.
8. I will not expand fast, no matter how successful I may be. I will remain prepared to pull out *at any time.*

SUCCESS DIAL 2

THE PAST MISTAKES I MADE THAT CAUSED ME TO FAIL

1. I ventured too deeply before I had enough experience. I didn't have enough "novice luck."
2. I did not check up thoroughly enough before making my moves. So, I was not prepared for what happened from making the wrong ones.
3. I did not seek a legal opinion when the venture was *for* profit.
4. I had enough funds to carry me through a bad beginning, but I used them up by expanding too fast.
5. By expanding too fast, besides, I did not save enough funds from my profits to carry me through unexpected upsets.
6. I expected a god in my partner. (Or, I let sentiment rule me in selecting him.) (Or I didn't take his cautioning seriously enough—to our mutual regret.)
7. I gave up too soon because my efforts brought only losses.
8. I was so successful at first that I expanded too fast by investing all my profits in the venture—and could not pull out when I should have.

SUCCESS DIAL 3

STEPS THE SUCCESSFUL PERSON WOULD NOT TAKE—
BUT WHICH I TOOK—AND FAILED

1. I let my overenthused physiological language make me throw caution to the winds.
2. I gave up at the first sign of failure, because my dejected physiological language took all the spirit out of me.
3. I was a mediocre success only because my relieved physiological language induced me to stop "straining" my brains.
4. I prattled my best plans to the "whole world" because my revelling physiological language filled me with overconfidence.
5. I underrated my competitors and shut my eyes to their true abilities.
6. I browbeat my partner or my counsellors whenever they didn't agree with me and see the "gem" of my ideas.
7. I underrated myself when my stunned physiological language did not recover swiftly enough from an unexpected failure.

SUCCESS DIAL 4

THE PRACTICAL WAY FOR ME TO
BRING ABOUT MY GOAL,
DREAM OR WISH

1. I'll be satisfied to achieve a moderate success in a certain period of time, and I won't let my enthusiasm to get rich quick (or to attain any other successes) enslave me to an ecstatic physiological language that will thrust all caution aside, should I succeed fast.
2. I have given my project a great deal of thought, and conducted thorough investigations. (Or I have not done enough of either, particularly in my branch of the venture—or in the region I plan to move to. I have to do still more.)
3. I have considered the legal pitfalls ahead by thoroughly looking them up in the library. I have also consulted with an attorney about my particular slant. (Or I have inquired from the place I plan to move to about its statutes concerning my venture.)
4. I have saved enough money for the venture, or can raise the rest with little borrowing. (This applies to whether I am going into business, buying stocks, or any other property.)
5. I have selected my partner. I know him long enough and am convinced that he is level-headed and not envious. Even in little things I have found him fair and square and honest. He also has stick-to-itiveness.

SUCCESS DIAL 5

THE MOST OPTIMISTIC WAY FOR ME TO
PURSUE MY GOAL, DREAM OR WISH

1. I am so confident that I will "strike it rich" (or climb high socially, or achieve whatever I seek) that I am going after it all-out from the very beginning.
2. I don't have to check up in detail before making a move. This venture can't miss! I see its big opportunities ahead! It *can't* fail! Why waste time preparing for possible disaster?
3. Why check with a lawyer? What is there to check? Everything I'm going to do is legal! Lawyers charge too much, anyhow! I can use that money better by investing it in my venture!
4. I don't need extra money to carry me through a bad beginning! This thing just can't fail! Too much caution, anyhow, annihilates ambition! Why should I clip my wings?
5. I know I have the right partner! He does everything I tell him to! He *knows* I can't fail! (Or, what do I need a partner for? Why make *somebody else* rich off *my* brains?)
6. I have the knack of success because I instinctively do things right! Why waste time and energy beating about the bush with endless reasoning?
7. I will expand fast and hit the iron while it's hot and zoom to the top! I'll borrow all I need, besides, for I'll pay it back in a jiffy with my profits!

SUCCESS DIAL 6

THE MOST PESSIMISTIC WAY FOR ME TO
PURSUE MY GOAL, DREAM OR WISH

1. I better wait much longer before getting into action. It takes far longer than I suspected to get experience for this undertaking. I am the "bad luck kid" or "Calamity Jane."
2. I better check up a lot more before making a move. Suppose everything goes wrong? I'll need a big sum of money to save me!
3. To play safe, I better consult five or six lawyers and get their opinions. The best lawyers could be wrong! (This includes lawyers, dentists, doctors, architects, reliable services, or experts in whatever you need to prepare you for your venture.)
4. I have to save *a lot more money* before starting. If I had a bad beginning, I'd never get out from under, otherwise!
5. I'll need a lot more money, too, to meet unexpected upsets. Shocking surprises are always ahead.
6. I need at least two or three partners *who really know their onions.* (Or, I wouldn't trust *any* partner! He could run off and leave me holding the empty bag! Or he could be too impractical!)
7. At the first sign of failure, I'll sell out! Why step deeper in the quicksand?
8. I'll wait a long time before expanding. Even then, I will do so *only slightly!* Better to keep the profits safely in the bank! I'll always be that much ahead then, if everything collapses, which it could do *any day!*

SUCCESS DIAL 7

WHAT WILL MOST PROBABLY HAPPEN IN ANY MOVE
I MAKE TOWARD A MONEY-MAKING GOAL

1. I'll discover that it requires more money to put across than I figured. The cost of everything I need, use or employ, seems hard to keep down.
2. Competition is stronger than I anticipated, mainly because others are already established, possess better equipment, more and better employees (if I have any), or even surprising cleverness and ease (if it is in social or romantic life).
3. The number of legal restrictions in my path astonish me.
4. My approach has to be constantly reslanted to fit the changing times. That forces me to watch the life scene closely.
5. I am always behind my "making big money" schedule and grow discouraged repeatedly.
6. Every time I make some good profits, I have to lay out for more supplies.
7. What I considered of minor importance before, I find most important now, such as, the weather and the distance. They inconvenience me greatly and waste too much of my valuable time (and cut into my reduced leisure time, too).
8. As I expand—or even build up my inventory—I find that my quarters are restricting. But I can't afford bigger ones yet. Nor am I sure if doing so would be wise until I am more soundly established in the venture.
9. The more my assets grow, the more vulnerable I am to losses, both physical and legal. Many of the most valuable assets of any enterprise, anyhow, (assets like names and addresses, scribbled notes with profitable ideas, experimental data, partly perfected inventions, potentially profitable creations, etc.) cannot be insured for anything near true value.
10. My wife (or husband) or family aren't cooperating with me as much as I had counted on. They are easily discouraged, too.

SUCCESS DIAL 8

HOW TO PREPARE MYSELF TO MEET ANY OF
THE EXIGENCIES OF SUCCESS DIAL 7
BEFORE I MAKE A MOVE

1. List and price the apparent expenditures ahead and maintain a surplus of 40 to 50 percent in funds.
2. Have something quaintly different, more specialized, harder to find anywhere (even if in personality) than my competitors. I can then profit more from it. (If in personality, I will reap greater rewards in business, socially and romantically.)
3. Investigate thoroughly, on my own, *before* consulting a lawyer, every legal restriction to every phase of my undertaking. *Then* a lawyer can really help me. Don't leave it up to him to teach me the most elementary facts.
4. Start with an idea a little ahead of my times, and never forego that lead. *Never* fall in step with the times, nor lag behind them.
5. *Expect* my "making big money" to lag behind schedule.
6. Don't expect to be making a profit too soon. So, always retain extra cash to keep me going at least three extra months.
7. Investigate thoroughly the seemingly minor everyday chores, duties, obstacles, climate, etc., and appraise how much they will handicap me or slow me down or deplete my energy. (Even pursuing someone romantically too far away might be difficult.)
8. Plan carefully how to expand in the smallest quarters possible. So, don't overinvest in equipment or inventory for some time. Plan, too, to avoid clutter and confusion and loss of time searching for things. Keep careful files.
9. But don't save money by taking up cheap quarters subject to fires, floods, theft, neighborhood snooping, easy public view, etc. And make copies of novel ideas and put them in a safe-deposit box.
10. Keep a cheerful face through the worst to your wife, family or partner, if they are easily discouraged.

SUCCESS DIAL 9

WHAT WILL I DO IF THE *BEST* THING HAPPENED TO MY UNDERTAKING?

1. My physiological language will explode with joy. My heart will blast away like a piston, and my muscles will feel like giant springs, ready to leap like a prehistoric grasshopper.

2. I will start living it up at last! I will take all the trips I've hoped to, live where I've wished to, work when I want to, dress as I care to, entertain as I crave to, decorate my mate with jewels, get the expensive operation I've put off so long, procure a dazzling country estate, or a deluxe condominium, townhouse or whatever, buy speculative stock and get much richer fast, purchase the fancy boat I dream about, go back to college, or whatever else I wish for most. [*But think twice before you act.* Normalize your physiological language by folding your hands tightly together for one second first. If you are still in doubt, look closely again at Success Dial 4 (page 163).]

3. If I get the big promotion or opportunity I seek, I will make outstanding changes in the department (or in my duties) which will increase the company profits—and its appreciation of me as well.

4. If I marry the heiress I am pursuing, I will treat her very kindly and romantically and convince her that I didn't marry her for her money. And I'll study her family business closely and take part in it and stop being a husband in name only.

5. If I marry a rich man whom I like very much, I will treat him romantically and convince him that I didn't marry him for his wealth. I'll make myself indispensable to him. When he is the least bit ill, I will shower him with *special attention.*

6. I will expand my venture, but borrow very little. I will specialize *still more* to still remain *unique* in the field.

SUCCESS DIAL 10

WHAT WILL I DO IF THE *WORST* THING HAPPENED TO MY UNDERTAKING?

1. My physiological language will turn me into jelly. My heart will speed like mad, but weakly, and my muscles will turn cold and flabby with frustration.
2. I will feel as if my whole life is over. All my dreams will have failed. Everything I aspired to do with the gains, will be impossible. I will be considered a failure. My family and associates will look upon me as impractical wish-thinker. I will have to continue my drudging life without fantastic luxury and without lavishing gifts on those I hoped to reward. I will be enraged at all the time I wasted on the futile venture. I will be ready to "dump the whole thing" and give up. [*But think twice before you act*. Normalize your physiological language by folding your hands tightly together first. If you are still in doubt, look closely again at Success Dial 1 (page 162).]
3. If I do not get the big promotion or the opportunity I seek, I will normalize my physiological language and realize that I have to try again, or accept whatever I had before.
4. If I fail to marry the heiress I am pursuing, I will remind myself that I have lived up to now *without* her wealth; that if she is "above" me because of her money, I better forget her.
5. If I fail to marry the rich man I like very much, I will remind myself that I have existed up to now *without* his luxuries; that if he is outside my reach because of them, I can live without them.
6. Or I will limit my venture to only what is *profitable* in it and abandon what *isn't*—at least, until its earnings improve substantially. But I will not borrow much, if at all, and increase my debts. Better, indeed, to string out my surplus without impoverishing myself.

How to Trigger Your Wisest Future
Action with the Miracle Mind Magic Stimulator

When you yearn to achieve a much-cherished, but seemingly inaccessible goal, dream or wish, trigger the right physiological language for it with the Miracle Mind Magic Stimulator. Then plunge excitedly into the secret mental power for wisest future action and reach your goal swiftly and easily with the minimum handicaps to hold you back. So, practice and master the Miracle Mind Magic Stimulator for this unique secret mental power.

Sit alone in your room and visualize yourself pursuing your seemingly unattainable goal, dream or wish with absolute confidence of success. Let this confidence flood your whole body simply by imagining it doing so, and your heart will lose the flutter of the anxiety-sympathetics' domination that lessens its power. Your jumpy muscles will relax and you will feel fully adequate to carry out your plans to perfection. Hold that vision of yourself for five seconds. Now visualize yourself achieving your goal and maintain that vision for four seconds. Repeat that procedure three times, as you learned from practicing the Miracle Mind Magic Stimulator in Lesson 3. Intensify it each time, so that your body speaks the right physiological language for wisest future action.

Your hesitation will vanish, and you will be eager to use *the few steps* you need in any Success Dial to insure your easy, swift success, for you will be guided, at every move, by the secret mental power of *wisest future action.*

Below are case histories of people who used this secret mental power for every day profit. Profit from it even more than they.

*How Austin E. Led His Company Successfully
Through a Recession Layoff Crisis*

Hard times struck the factory where Austin E. was plant supervisor, and the fear of layoffs hung over the place. The plant laid off a number of workers to cut expenses. The rest of them, dreading a similar fate, slowed down to stretch out the work, and their absenteeism increased from ten to fifteen percent. The company tried to remove the scare by giving the doomed workers two or three weeks' notice, plus severance and vacation pay. But that did not help. "Whenever you lay off people," Austin told me in despair, "you develop a sense of insecurity in those who stay with you." He even wondered whether the factory itself could survive.

I taught him the secret mental power for wisest future action. Austin triggered it with the Miracle Mind Magic Stimulator and altered his anxiety-ridden physiological language into the right, confident one for this secret mental power. With it he used *the* step he needed from Success Dial 1 (page 162) to review his past mistakes and boldly analyzed how it could have avoided making them. He studied its present plans to ride through the crisis and applied Success Dial 5 (page 164) for the most optimistic way he could proceed with each plan. He checked it with Success Dial 6 (page 165) to compare it with the most pessimistic way he could proceed with each plan, and noted the best and the worst that could happen to his company. Austin's mind and body now spoke the right physiological language of confidence, and he outlined what he called "the fight to the last round" spirit.

He persuaded the company president to let him put them into action. Its aim was to prod the employees to work harder and the salesmen to sell more, at a time when the economy was alarmingly sluggish. The desperate president joined him in the plan and stood with him on a platform in front of the sales force and the work force, and the two of them led all the frightened employees in song. Both the president and Austin sang at the top of their voices, and pumped their arms and gesticulated vigorously with the best. They stimulated the employees with the joys of working for that firm.

The whole thing sounded asinine, Austin admitted to me. "But everybody got busy," he went on, and the company *successfully survived the hard times.* (It did, as I explained to Austin, because the "asinine" singing subdued the anxiety-sympathetics of the employees and normalized the panicky physiological language with which it dominated them.)

How Margaret U., a Poor Widow, Started a
Little Business and Tripled Her Profits in
a Year, and Retired Two Years Later

Margaret U. was left a poor widow at sixty-two when her husband succumbed from a heart attack. All she inherited was his comparatively small life insurance and his social security benefits. After subsisting for a while like the proverbial abandoned "old and poor" and grieving in loneliness and with a minimum of comfort, Margaret begged me for advice. I taught her the secret mental power for wisest future action.

She triggered it with the Miracle Mind Magic Stimulator and altered her anxiety-ridden physiological language into the right, confident one for this secret mental pᴏ⁻ ⸴. Then, with Success Dial 2 (page 162), she reviewed the mistakes which she and her husband had made during their lives (mistakes which had left them poor in their old age), and boldly analyzed how they could have avoided making those mistakes. With Success Dial 4 (page 163), she picked out her plans for survival, and prepared herself for every move in it with Success Dials 7 and 8 (pages 166, 167).

Her mind and body now spoke the right physiological language of confidence. Her plans for survival consisted in her undertaking something which she could handle efficiently, due to her past experience in keeping a home for her family and in taking care of her older parents. She proceeded with them and, by the end of the year, she had tripled her business and was earning more in one month than her husband had earned in six. Two years later Margaret sold out and put her multiplied capital gains in the bank and added the interest on it to her social security benefits. Margaret no longer lived like the abandoned "old and poor."

How William D. Fled from a Good Position He
Hated to a Much Smaller One He Loved, and
Soon Made Twice as Much Money

William D. was a highly-paid executive who lived in affluence in a suburb outside the big city where he worked. But he was dissatisfied with his position. The company was well-entrenched, but was near peak growth. Worse still, it could merge with another and endanger William's post! But even without that risk, it had grown staid and conventional and restrained William's daring and originality. The stockholders expected him now to fulfill more the duties of a manager than of a pioneer. But William yearned for the challenge and excitement of leading a tottering establishment out of danger and into surpassing its competitors. In his present job he felt like a caged animal with a distrustful keeper, and started drinking.

He made up his mind to change to a position that electrified him. Either that or lose his health and sanity. But how would he find it? If he changed to one that went downhill instead, he would be worse off. He did not relish a life of poverty for his family and himself, but one that offered thrilling rewards.

I taught William the secret mental power for wisest future action. With the Miracle Mind Magic Stimulator he triggered within him the right physiological language for wisest future action. He used Success Dial 1 (page 162) to guide him in selecting a position that offered him the challenge and excitement he sought. With Success Dial 5 (page 164) he looked at it with the most optimistic eyes. But, to avoid making a fool of himself, he immediately viewed it, with Success Dial 6 (page 165), with the most pessimistic eyes. At once he saw the pitfalls he would plunge into if he repeated past mistakes. To check on those mistakes he breezed over Success Dial 2 (page 162) and boldly analyzed how he could have avoided them. Had he taken another job rather than the one he had, he would be leading another company into newer adventures and making three times what he made now. He had chosen too secure a firm.

With both sides of the question clear before him now, William prepared thoroughly with step 2 of Success Dials 9 and 10 (pages 168, 169), for the best and the worst that could happen to him from his plans. Then he went into action.

He landed a position with a tottering company of a different type of business altogether. The big challenge and excitement—and the threat of failure—were all in it. William ceased drinking and applied himself feverishly to the problems of the establishment. Two years later he set it back on its feet, with big contracts ahead. So satisfied were the stockholders that they voted him a startling increase in pay and in stock options which totalled twice what he had received on his old job. And William had hardly tapped the future possibilities of the firm! Not only that, but he was enjoying to the hilt the very kind of life he wanted to live most!

How Grace N. Easily Brought Her Obstinate Husband Around to Her Way of Thinking Without Argument

Grace N. was a middle-aged woman and wanted to stay looking "young." She had been concerned with her figure ever since having her first child. She had two more since. Now they were grown up and married. But Grace deeply resented being practically shoved off the earth now that she was middle-aged and had lost the glamour of a young bride. A certain region of her anatomy looked particularly "old" and singled her out as a woman who was "getting on." But it could be corrected with plastic surgery. When Grace excitedly revealed that to Howard, he shot back a firm "No!"

Grace became desperate. The operation would not affect her health, except to leave her looking (and feeling) considerably younger. But Howard remained adamant and more or less implied that she ought to be satisfied to "get old gracefully."

At her insistence I taught her the secret mental power for wisest future action. She triggered it with the Miracle Mind Magic Stimulator and altered her anxiety-ridden physiological language into the right, confident one for this secret mental power. With steps 1, 2, 6 and 7 of Success Dial 2 (page 162) she understood why she failed in trying to influence her obstinate husband, and boldly analyzed how she could have avoided making her past mistakes. With steps 1 and 5 of Success Dial 4 (page 163) she saw how to change her husband's mind. Her mind and body at once spoke the right physiological language of confidence.

She would calmly but subtly entice Howard to feel that *he* wanted her to have that corrective operation. It involved the use of flirtation and other enthralling wiles, rather than logic and argument.

SUMMARY OF THIS SECRET MENTAL POWER

With wisest future action you pick out the most effective way to go after anything *before you even make a move.* Usually with no more than a single step or two of the Success Dial which obviously fits your case, you foresee the unsuspected difficulties and hidden perils in whatever you undertake and avoid being caught by surprise. You are, therefore, fully prepared to extricate yourself from any calamity that might overtake you in anything. You are guaranteed success in achieving your goal, dream or wish. Other Success Dials double this guarantee by showing you how. To acquire this secret mental power quickly and easily, follow these simple routines:

1. With the Miracle Mind Magic Stimulator trigger in you the right physiological language for wisest future action.
2. Then look at the steps of Success Dial 1 (page 162) to find out what step (or steps) the person who succeeded where you failed followed to achieve your goal, dream or wish.
3. Then look at Success Dial 2 (page 162) for the past mistakes which caused you to fail.
4. Boldly analyze how you could have avoided making those mistakes.
5. Look at Success Dial 4 (page 163) for the practical way to bring about your pressing goal, dream or wish.
6. If you are timid about it, spin yourself into action with any one step in Success Dial 5 (page 164).
7. In case you are too blindly optimistic before you are ready, restrain yourself somewhat with any step of Success Dial 6 (page 165).
8. If it is a money-making venture, make Success Dials 7 and 8 (pages 166, 167) your "bible" for every step you make.
9. After you are in action and are succeeding, gain the most from your efforts with Success Dial 9 (page 168).
10. After you are in action, but should you not be doing as well as expected, rectify your course and speed on to your goal with Success Dial 10 (page 169).

You are now ready to use the miracle of the Success Dial to make every goal, dream or wish come true without "pull" and with the least effort on your part.

Lesson 14

The Secret Mental Power
to Time Your Actions Perfectly

No matter how well you apply all the previous secret mental powers, you may still fail miserably unless you time their uses favorably. But you can magnify their effects astronomically if you time them perfectly in life. *This* secret mental power, then, is *the great effortless multiplier of results in everything you undertake.* You don't have to strain a bit more when you use it, but everything you do with it, every move you make, every investment you get into, every attempt of yours at anything in life, carries the magic stamp of swift, easy, undeniable success. Closed social doors swing wide open. Unreachable opportunities beg to be seized. Unattainable romantic partners pursue you. Joys await you everywhere. The envied promotion, the big contract, the long-awaited fortune—they are all yours for the taking. With such effortless achievement your body speaks the right physiological language, and that converts you into *a genius in action in anything and everything.* You are unstoppable, invincible, undiscourageable, for all your barriers are torn down. All because you now time your moves perfectly. You sail now *with* the stream, not against it. You take the tide at the flood, as Shakespeare wrote, and it hurls you into fame and fortune. *Master this secret mental power!* Nothing earthly can reward you more!

The Fantastic Profits from Timing
Perfectly in Life

The profits from timing perfectly in life are so fantastic that everybody is aware of them. With perfect timing, certain people, with but a few dollars, skyrocketed into the multimillionaire class in an incredibly short time. Others made fortunes swiftly in the stock market. Revolutionary leaders with ill-armed, untrained men, vanquished heavily-armed, well-trained armies (Washington and countless others). Men with little chance of victory ascended to the Presidency (Lincoln). Women with little opportunity married financial tycoons. Outclassed, soft-punching boxers knocked out champions with one blow. Small teams of young, virtually inexperienced musicians reaped millions in a few years. Amateur realtors grew rich in staggeringly short periods, as did inexperienced salesmen. Crude writers broke best-seller records. Men in sackcloth changed the course of history (like Peter the Hermit who sparked the Crusades, and others). The list is endless. Nothing guarantees success easier and faster than the right timing. It shoves you ahead with the natural push of the times. Take full advantage of this secret mental power and let the *times work for you*, instead of *you against the times*.

The Magic of Perfect Timing in Life

In every move you make in life, timing is a primary factor. Without it you can accomplish little, no matter how hard you try. Even your breathing, your heartbeat, your movements, your walking, eating, talking—all depend upon proper timing. With improper muscle timing you stumble when you walk, choke when you swallow, stutter when you talk. In romantic conquest, in seeking a friend or making a transaction, timing is of paramount importance for success. Without it an athlete cannot get far; a boxer would miss or land only "lucky" punches, a musician could not carry a tune, a soldier could not carry out battle orders. Even strikes and protests have to be perfectly timed to be effective. To act a little too soon, or a little too late, will wreck the best-prepared plans. And a miss is as "good" as a mile.

In more intellectual fields, like art, science, and the professions, perfect timing is again the decisive factor. The Beatles achieved their phenomenal success by devising a new beat—or a new timing to their music. It differed from the classical timing by turning off into a surprising twist just when one expected to hear the conventional note. Others followed in their wake and amassed millions, too. The Beatles also timed their music to answer the silent call of the younger generation for something new and different. Their whole success was a masterpiece of perfect timing in life.

Even the magician has to perform his tricks with perfect timing of his hands, facial expressions, and body movements, to mislead the keenest observer. He must appear to do one thing, but actually do the opposite. Even in lovemaking, in fact, perfect timing is of the utmost importance. What will thrill your mate at one time won't necessarily do so at another. Even jokes have to be perfectly timed, or they might only insult or infuriate.

The Magic of Perfect Timing in Business

In business, you have to make thorough plans and subject them to immediate change when necessary. You have to keep abreast of major changes in world and national affairs, and of major and minor changes in your own field or in rival fields which can indirectly affect your own. Your prospects of business growth depend upon your making wise decisions at the right moments and from measuring your gains mainly from the long-range view. You have to time your promoting, advertising, and distributing to the most favorable periods of the year, to the demands of the regions you do business with, to public prejudice, and to the changing times. A superlative sales angle of a year ago might fizzle today due to a drastic change in public policy, to the occurrence of an important event, or even to public boredom toward that "old" approach.

On the other hand, you can't present an angle that is beyond the present knowledge and acceptance of the patronizing public. Your knowing what is "good" for people will bring you few sales if the buying public has not been educated to accept your valuable knowledge as true. It takes ten years for a novel idea to be accepted by the general public. When science disproves an accepted theory, only a microscopic fraction of the public reads or hears about it at first. A still smaller fraction accepts or remembers it. The overwhelming majority of the population does not even hear about it for years. The new idea, meanwhile, is likely to disappear from the public mind altogether, unless it is blazoned away by advertisements or in statements by publicity seekers. Before it can gain enough universal acceptance for you to prosper from it, about ten years of constantly hammering it into the public's mind by advertisements or authorities must elapse. Otherwise your investment is a poor risk and will require a massive supply of capital to push, or it will fail altogether.

A wise businessman cautiously tackles an entirely new idea. He promotes, instead, a modified form of it which is accepted by the times. He modifies this form of it years later to a more advanced form, before too many others leap into the field. Not until many years have passed does he dare to push the original, revolutionary form of the idea. With such perfect timing, he saves his head from battering against the stone wall of a too resistant market, as well as the legal perils of being challenged to prove the truth of his assertions to different governmental bodies.

Ill-Timed, Shackling Introspection, and How to Prevent It from Ruining Your Opportunities

No obstacle ruins your opportunities socially and romantically, and even in business, so fatally and senselessly as ill-timed, shackling introspection. Time and again when you have the right opportunity to make a valuable contact, to make a tremendous impression, to win the mate you want, to strike it right in business, to utter the right word or make the right move to win the big chance in whatever you have waited or prepared for, you hesitate, shackled by doubting, ill-timed introspection, and let the opportunity of your lifetime slip through your fingers. You feel like kicking yourself afterward for the hesitancy—*after* your greatest chance has gone, perhaps never to return. Other chances do come, but your ill-timed, shackling introspection ruins them again and again. You seem unable to cast off this curse.

Ill-timed, shackling introspection consists of suddenly losing all confidence in your ability to win somebody, to perform a skill expertly, or to perform capably *anything* for which you are *thoroughly prepared* beforehand. It overcomes you with terror, and your fear-sympathetics rout your normal physiological language and throw your heart into wild beating, and freezes (hypertones) your muscles into helplessness. You just stand there, a thick lump in your throat, your stomach fluttering, your knees trembling, and your body breaking out in a cold sweat. Suddenly realizing that you have botched your big opportunity, panic grips you and your heart bombards your chest. Your blood pressure bolts up thirty to fifty points higher, or more. You have been converted into a physiological language lunatic, all because of your ill-timed, shackling introspection.

How to Oust the Crippling Physiological
Language of Ill-Timed, Shackling Introspection

You can still save your big opportunity by ousting this lunatic physiological language. Do so by lowering your blood pressure swiftly. Its sudden rise enslaved you with that undesirable physiological language. But since it rose through wrong introspection, you can lower it again with *right* introspection. The magic tool for that is the "thought plateau." Like a plateau, which is an elevated tract of *level land* at the foot of a mountain, the "thought plateau" rapidly brings your blood pressure down again almost to normal and maintains it there.

This is how the thought-plateau operates. Physiologists have discovered that you *can* learn conscious control of normally unconscious phenomena, like blood pressure, without becoming a Yogi. When your blood pressure suddenly rises, as it does with ill-timed, shackling introspection, it means that your fear-sympathetics have *narrowed* your smaller arteries by contracting the circular muscles in their walls. To lower such a blood pressure, you have to *relax* those circular muscles.

You can relax them at will by listening to your brain waves when your blood pressure is up, and forcibly thinking of their sounds when your blood pressure is down. That can be done with a brain-wave machine. But since you can't go around in public with such a cumbersome device attached to your head, you practice with it in private and memorize the sounds of your brain waves when your blood pressure is high, and when it is normal. You then lower your blood pressure when it is high by reproducing in your mind the brain-wave sounds of normal blood pressure.

The magical "thought plateau" does likewise for you more easily, inexpensively, and without possible side effects. So master this miraculous secret.

The Magical "Thought Plateau" to Lower the Blood Pressure of Your Crippled Physiological Language at Will

Sit quietly and comfortably in your room and close your eyes. Grow thoroughly aware of your natural feelings as you sit there. Be aware of how relaxed you feel, for "all" your muscles are at ease. The circular muscles of your small arteries respond, reflexively, by relaxing too, and your blood pressure falls, That's why you are asked to sit down and relax for a while before your blood pressure is taken by a doctor. Although you don't hear your brain waves then, they are sounding a low (or lower) blood pressure note. Whenever you feel *as you do then*, in other words (*fully relaxed and even slightly drowsy*), accept the fact that your blood pressure is *low* (for you) and that your brain waves are sounding its note.

Think, next, of some big opportunity ahead, waiting for you. Visualize yourself facing it and ready to seize it, but suddenly finding yourself *incapable* of doing so. (Visualize *any* big opportunity you wish, be it social, romantic, business, or whatever.) Visualize this scene so *realistically* that you are gripped with the terror of losing the big chance for which you waited so long. Visualize it so realistically that your fear-sympathetics upset your normal physiological language and paralyze you with dread. The more realistically you visualize this scene, the more paralyzed with dread you will feel.

Your muscles will no longer be relaxed, but will overtense, ready to spring into flight. The circular muscles of your small arteries will respond reflexly and overtense, too, and skyrocket your blood pressure by as much as thirty to fifty points. Make yourself keenly aware of the "tightness" gripping you all over now—aware of the feeling of being frozen into helplessness. Your brain waves are then sounding the notes of high blood pressure (for you). You don't have to hear them to know that they are. *They always sound that note whenever you put yourself in that state*!

To lower that heightened blood pressure, just *relax* the circular muscles of the walls of your small arteries. To do so, simply visualize yourself feeling again *just as you did* when you first sat down and grew thoroughly aware of how relaxed you felt. Your brain waves will start sounding the note of low blood pressure, and the circular muscles of your small arteries will relax, reflexly, with your big muscles. Your blood pressure will automatically drop back to normal.

That is the magic of the "thought plateau." With a little practice you can do it at will, any time, anywhere! You will then always oust the crippling physiological language of ill-timed, shackling introspection, and use the secret mental power of perfect timing in life. Master the *"thought plateau."*

How to Trigger Perfect Timing with the Miracle Mind Magic Stimulator

Your great difficulty in using perfect timing is the innate inertia in your brain against disciplining itself into applying it. With perfect timing you seldom respond effusively and plunge into action the moment an impulse strikes you, unless you have prepared for it. With perfect timing you have to do the right thing, no matter how eager you may be to do something entirely different. The Miracle Mind Magic Stimulator puts you into that "right mood" by throwing you into the right physiological language for it. Your heartbeat, your breathing and metabolic rates, your muscle tone, your digestion and assimilation, the blood flow to your brain, all change then to enable you to function in the most efficient manner, with the least waste of physical or emotional energy. Your conscious mind then revels with the thrill and confidence of easy achievement.

This is how to practice and master the Miracle Mind Magic Stimulator for this secret mental power. Sit alone in your room and visualize the achievement, the venture, the conquest, the rewards, the victory, or whatever else you long for from this secret mental power. That is your goal, dream, or wish. Hold that picture in your mind for five seconds.

Then visualize your goal as coming true; visualize yourself always making the right move in sports competition, in playing a musical instrument, in business, in romance, in social climbing, in running for office, or in anything whatsoever. Visualize yourself doing it as perfectly as such a person would. Maintain that vision for four seconds.

Repeat that procedure three times, as you learned from practicing the Miracle Mind Magic Stimulator in Lesson 3. Intensify it each item, so you actually visualize yourself changing into *the kind of person* who achieves your goal, dream, or wish with ease and perfection. Practice acquiring this feeling of *becoming such a person* until your nerves tingle with eagerness to achieve exactly what he does. Practice it until you need to visualize it just once, in two seconds, for your physiological language to alter and speak like his! You will be ready to trigger the secret mental power of perfect timing in life swiftly thereafter.

Below are case histories of people who used this secret mental power for everyday profit. Their names have been changed. Study them well and do even better yourself in similar circumstances.

How Fifty-One-Year-Old Sheila C. Accurately
Foresaw for the Future a Delightful,
$20,000-a-Year Part-Time Self-Employment
Career for Which She Could Prepare in Her
Spare Time

Sheila C. did not mind her work, but it was tiresome and repetitious, and lacked variety. But every job, she concluded, had its drawbacks. Besides, to learn a new one at her age seemed impractical. And yet she would not qualify for social security for years. Even then, she could not live on it as she did on her wages. She would have to continue working, no matter how much her job bored her. Should her company compel her to retire, though, her standard of living would be seriously upset.

For these and many other reasons, Sheila sought desperately for something she liked doing which she could learn on her own, and which could bring her enough to maintain her present style of life. But she couldn't decide what to select.

I taught her the secret mental power to time perfectly in life. With the magic of perfect timing in business she compared several prospective skills with each other, but could not make up her mind. With the Miracle Mind Magic Stimulator, however, she acquired the right physiological language for perfect timing in life and compared these different skills again. This time she promptly discarded some which were in demand at the time by realizing that they might not be in such demand ten years in the future. The words, "It takes ten years for a new idea to be accepted by the general public," fastened on her mind and harmonized with her acquired right physiological language. And so, she picked a skill whose scientific basis, at that time, was viewed with skepticism.

Sheila studied it in her spare time and, in a few months, was so proficient with it that she used it for people. Demands for her services grew, and after several years she was earning $18,000 annually from it, *part-time* (or twice her working wages) *and in the privacy of her home.*

How Elmer Q. Easily and Quickly Achieved
His Seemingly Impossible Greatest Wish

Elmer Q. held his MBA job for twenty years and was growing sick of it. During that time he was left behind by dozens of "job-hoppers" in his firm, and he felt like a coward. He seethed with jealousy when new employees secretly worked there just long enough to acquire "additional training or experience" and suddenly disappeared into big jobs or opened their own establishments. Agnes, his wife, did not complain, but Elmer considered himself a big disappointment.

So he made up his mind to take action. He was getting no younger, he reminded himself. He had to make the break now, for he ached to travel on his job. But he couldn't decide when to make the break.

I taught Elmer the secret mental power to time perfectly in life. With the Miracle Mind Magic Stimulator, he triggered in himself the right physiological language for it. Then he studied the situation carefully and faced boldly the fact that, in a survey of over 5,000 holders of MBA degrees, most of those who had changed jobs from three to five times in the last five years were being paid no more now than those who had not! But that did not satisfy him. He wanted to change into a much better job.

He applied to a much bigger company, but when he faced its head, ill-timed, shackling introspection froze him like a statue. With the "thought plateau," though, he lowered his blood pressure, freed himself from the crippling physiological language, and declaimed like someone who could bring the firm a great future. He was hired on the spot. Elmer soon impressed his new superior so tremendously that he was rewarded with a special assignment and a thrilling increase in pay.

How Hector K. Grew Rich Easily by Calculating His Company's Best Business Move Like a Seer

Hector K. was the manager of special projects of the company he worked for. With the firm's earnings depressed for some time, Hector's stock options amounted to little. But he liked his job and the company, and was determined that it prosper once again. Its only hope, as he saw it, was to "take the plunge" and launch a new, but successful, product.

To put a new product on the market, though, was costly, complicated, and risky. Thousands of new products were launched by different establishments in the nation every year, and the number was increasing. But their chances of success were mixed at best. A survey revealed that three out of every ten "major" new products introduced by different companies in the previous five years had failed to sell as expected, and one out of ten had done so poorly that it had to be withdrawn. Only one of twelve ideas brought to a firm was worth testing, and but one out of every four tested wound up being made into profitable products. A flop, too, was little enhancement for the reputation of the executive who pushed it. So Hector realized that he would be jeopardizing his whole future in the concern, as well as the concern itself, if he sponsored the wrong product.

Scared as to what best to do, he asked me for help. I taught him the secret mental power to time perfectly in life. Hector mastered it in a couple of days. With the Miracle Mind Magic Stimulator he normalized his physiological language into the right one for this secret mental power. He then coolly admitted to himself that actual differences between many products were so small that a big number of buyers had trouble distinguishing which product was better than the other. The product, instead, had to be unique, so that people would be willing to try it. And it had to be priced right. Hector disliked heatedly a new fad which was gripping the young. But with his right physiological language to time perfectly in life he envisioned that fad catching on widely in a year or two.

That provided Hector with the clue to the unique name and to the advertising appeal for his new product. By controlling the ill-timed shackling introspection which nearly ruined his opportunity to convince his company's conference board for his product idea, he won its approval for it. The product was brought out. It made a hit. Hector's stock options rose fast in value and doubled his wealth.

SUMMARY OF THIS SECRET MENTAL POWER

To time perfectly in life is to reduce the time and effort you have to spend attaining anything, to a minimum bordering on the miraculous. No matter how well prepared you are to achieve any goal, dream, or wish, you might *never* achieve it unless you time it perfectly in life. To acquire this secret mental power, follow these simple routines:

1. When you are prepared to venture into anything, trigger the secret mental power to time perfectly in life with the Miracle Mind Magic Stimulator, so your body will speak the right physiological language for it.
2. Then analyze it carefully with the magic of perfect timing in life, or in business, to make sure that the time for your venture is appropriate.
3. Once your decision is made but you are seized by the crippling physiological language of ill-timed, shackling introspection, oust it by lowering your skyrocketing blood pressure with the magical "thought plateau."
4. Then succeed miraculously and quickly with your venture.

Lesson 15

Secret Mental Power to Rout Your Nagging Aches and Minor Illness

No matter how completely you proceed to achieve your goal, dream, or wish—indeed, even *after* you achieve it—your every gain or pleasure from it will be ruined if you are afflicted with nagging aches and minor illness. The constant irritations, both physical and mental, resulting from them will harass you continually and draw your attention away from your newly-won joys. They turn you inward into the darkness of your miserable body and convert you into a grouchy crab. They supersensitize you to their ever-reminding tortures, leaving you increasingly aware of them, even if their discomforts grow no worse.

Your much-cherished goal is superseded in your thinking by an abnormal concentration on your persistent sufferings. Family and friends find your company less and less pleasurable. The nagging pains and your helpless engrossment in them tighten the muscles of your brows and cheeks, and endow you with the haggard mien of the emotionally unstable misanthropist.

Your physiological language, as a result, speaks a bitter, fight-sympathetics language and your blood pressure rises, due to your mental tension and speeded-up heartbeat. The muscles in the region of the nagging pain are thrown into spasm and intensify your misery. The muscles of your whole body, in fact, are hypertensed, subconsciously, in fury against the insistent aches.

Minor illness, like headaches, affect you likewise. And so, you are converted into a near madman—even if you have achieved your greatest goals, dreams, or wishes. If you haven't achieved them yet, you hardly will against such merciless handicaps. Master the secret mental power to rout nagging pains and minor illness if you expect to truly gain anything out of life, even if everything is thrown into your lap.

The Fantastic Profits from Routing
Nagging Aches and Minor Illness

The profits from routing nagging aches and minor illness are unlimited because nothing can hold you back more than such handicaps. By routing them, people have changed instantly from "impossible" into super-popular individuals. Others who were getting nowhere suddenly surged ahead of everybody else.

Romantic mates, on the brink of being deserted or divorced, were suddenly worshipped and slaved for. Hypochondriacs who were given up as incurable suddenly healed themselves. People driven to the borderline of suicide suddenly took hold of themselves and adjusted contentedly to the world. Individuals who looked and felt twenty to thirty years older than they were regained their youth. People who could not enjoy their leisure time or their retirement started enjoying them like children. Failures in art, writing, inventing, music, acting, or in hobbies, like golf, attained remarkable successes.

The list is endless of how people completely changed their lives by routing their nagging aches and minor illness. Master this lesson and reach your goals, and revel in them to the full.

How Your Everyday Bad Habits Can Bring on
Nagging Aches and Minor Illness

Your everyday bad habits (like bad posture, bad dietary habits, and daily tensions) can bring on nagging aches and minor illness so subtly that you aren't aware of them until you are suddenly half-crippled by them. Your everyday bad habits constitute a form of minor trauma which you regularly deal yourself. Your body seems unaffected by them at first, for they cause only slight discomforts which your sensory nerves hardly convey to your conscious mind. They are still affecting your body or your organs in one way or another, nonetheless, and building up an explosive physiological state. If you are very sensitive by nature (such as, if you naturally possess an unusual number of sensory nerves throughout your body), you will feel the effects sooner than if you are less sensitive by nature. Whichever you are, though, one day, with little warning, you grow conscious of a nagging pain or annoying discomfort in some part of your body, and your troubles have begun. You try to ignore it, but it distracts your attention from your significant problems. You are thrown into anger and frustration, and that alters your physiological language, and your whole personality as well.

How Your Daily Unsuspected Bad Posture Can Bring on Nagging Aches and Minor Illness

After you stop growing, the curvature of your back increases an average of fifteen degrees, according to Dr. Dennis K. Collins of the University of Iowa Hospital Department of Orthopedic Surgery. Ninety percent of the middle-aged patients he followed up continued to live normal lives as best as they could, without surgery, and confined their treatment to exercises and braces. Such typical patients are actually plagued with nagging aches and minor illnesses until periodically relieved by the treatments. But the treatments cannot perform miracles for them because the primary cause of their abnormal back curvatures remained; that is, their bad posture.

But you can't spend all day long staring at yourself in a mirror to see that your posture is always right. Even if it were you might overextend the joints of your back and hips in one way or another by lifting something too heavy for you, or by lifting something light enough from a difficult position to grasp firmly while keeping your back straight, or by sitting too long in bad posture chairs, or by sitting in any chair until you tire and sag into bad posture.

You might strain your back, like a housewife or a grandmother, simply by helping with a baby or a pet; or even by working around the house, or hauling your shopping, or caring for an invalid relative. Even driving your car too long in one position can develop a condition approaching "driver's sciatica." Whatever the reasons, your back curves increasingly with time. You may suffer no discomfort for years, but eventually the bend in your back becomes acute enough to press just hard enough upon the nerves passing in or out of its different openings to torment you with vague, nagging pains.

These, in time, can lead to minor illnesses resembling rheumatism, digestive disturbances, headaches, or backaches. They baffle your doctor, for they are puzzling to diagnose. Yet they alter your physiological language into a morbid one, and ruin you as a person and in your career by affixing themselves on your conscious mind.

How Your Common Dietary Habits Can Bring on Nagging Aches and Minor Illness

Your common dietary habits can afflict you with nagging pains and minor illness. The very teasing from your family, friends, and associates that you are acquiring a "pot belly" secretly vexes you and changes your physiological language into a pugnacious one, especially if you can't resist sweets or fattening foods. Fatty foods, besides, digest slowly and keep your stomach secreting digestive acid for up to five hours. If you regularly consume fried foods, pork, bacon, eggs, cheese, most nuts, whole milk, butter, desserts, ice cream and other icy and creamed products, candy, chocolate, pies and cream, soft drinks and liquors, and so forth, your stomach will regularly contain, for hours at a time, excess gastric juices. Your gastric glands, in turn, hypertrophy to fill the abnormal demand, and you acquire an "acid" stomach. You belch to raise the resulting gas and relieve the miserable discomfort of heartburn (the excessive pocket of gas in your stomach pressing against the lower end of your heart). You are plagued with recurring headaches, and with resisting bowels which aggravate them. The headaches may push into the top of your head, slightly to the left side, and move straight forward, toward your forehead. Or they might alternate to a disturbing fluttering on your temples.

The unavoidable physical movements and bending during

your work, when your stomach is still digesting a meal (such as, after lunch), draws digesting blood away from it and encourages a degree of indigestion (or digestion stoppage). Your stomach then either floods itself with still more gastric juices in an effort to resume your normal digestion, or it partially tightens its openings and retains the slowly digesting food within it longer than normally. Some of that food, as a consequence, putrefies and dumps some toxin into your bloodstream, and causes vague headache. All this leaves your physiological language unstable and curses you with nagging aches and minor illness.

How Your Daily Tensions Can Bring on Nagging Pains and Minor Illness

Dr. Henry I. Russek, noted New York cardiologist, like so many others, points out that "stressful life experiences" can directly and indirectly lead to arteriosclerosis (hardening of the arteries). Tension headaches represent reactions to stress; that is, to emotional stress. (But stress can also be physical, like that resulting from bad posture.) Forty percent of those who suffer from tension headaches suffer from a pain caused by the continuous contraction of head and neck muscles in response to stress. A head or neck muscle is a muscle, like an arm muscle, and it can ache like one. It also squeezes the arteries beneath it and reduces its own blood supply. A muscle pain may last for hours, days, or weeks, commonly either on both sides of the head or in the back of it, above the neck. It may even travel to the face or encircle the head, like a hatband. Bad posture can cause a similar headache. So can tension, by fixing your head, without your suspecting it, into the posture of the poised animal ready to defend itself. When your daily tension is assumed regularly, your neck retains that posture regularly.

Other muscles of your body tense, too, with your daily tension, although they don't pester you with headaches. When you lie down to rest, for example, you will discover that your hands, arms, shoulders, and legs are also tense. Not until you are reclining for some time will they relax. Indirectly, though, they also contribute to your vague headaches by retaining too much blood in them and starving your brain of its normal blood supply and consequent necessary oxygen. They do likewise to your stomach and alimentary canal and encourage indigestion, all of which upsets your physiological language.

How to Change Your Daily, Unsuspected Bad Posture That Brings on Nagging Pains and Minor Illness

Dr. Murray M. Braaf, director of the headache clinic at Stuyvesant Hospital, New York, found in a study of 100 headache-prone children, ages eight to sixteen, that stretching the neck with gentle traction produced cures in most of them. Most headaches in children and adults, he believed, arose from childhood injuries received and forgotten but resulting in changes in the curvature of the back and affecting the neck ligaments. By stretching the neck for thirty minutes three times a week, the doctor discovered, "permanent relief can be obtained."

Stretching the neck (and the spine, too, for the neck is a prolongation of the back) relieves the headache due to bad posture, whether encouraged by a forgotten childhood injury or by bad posture. In either case the contracted muscles of the neck are stretched and their spasms "eased out." Their blood flow returns to normal, and the muscles stop issuing pain-calls for more oxygen.

Since bad posture ever threatens you, however, and since you probably lack the time and patience to stretch your muscles regularly, you can achieve satisfactory results with a *simple thought*. That's how to use the secret mental power to rout your nagging pains and minor illness.

The Simple Thought to Change Your Unsuspected Bad Posture That Brings on Nagging Pains and Minor Illness

Whenever you stand, walk, or sit, visualize every now and then a sharp spike tied to your chest (See Illustration 15-1) pointing up to below your chin. Imagine its pointed end stabbing into the bottom of your chin whenever you slouch. Practice it a few times at home by using your index finger for the spike, to get used to being jabbed from below whenever your posture is bad.

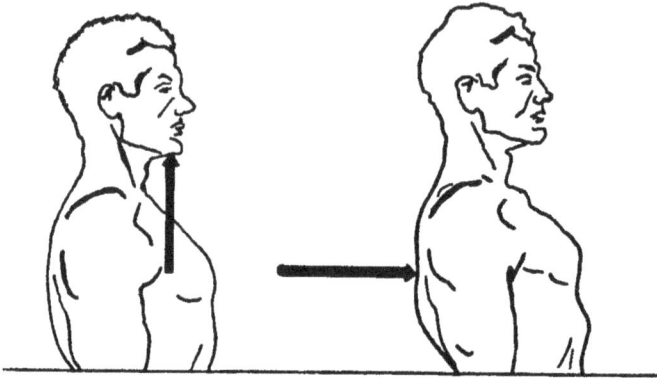

Illustration 15-1

At the same time, visualize another spike pointing at you from behind, at the upper part of your back, so that it stabs into your back every time you stop walking, sitting, or standing *tall.* (Illustration 15-1.)

Practice these two simple thoughts *at the same time* and make them *one.* They will automatically sit or stand you up straight every time you droop forward. If you are suffering from a posture backache, it will relieve it in no time. Make it your invisbile, healthy "headache pill"—*without side effects.*

How to Nullify Your Daily Tensions That Bring on Nagging Aches and Minor Illness

Life is full of daily tensions. Whenever you relieve one, another one takes its place, for there is no end to their number. Even the wealthy man, who is buried in money, worries about the service he receives from his help; his departing youth; whether people like him for himself or for his gold; whether "everybody" is trying to swindle him, and so on. To those who possess little riches, such a man's tensions are ludicrous; but to *him* they are as upsetting as big bills are to a poor man. His life, too, may be boring to him because he has really so little to worry about that he goes frantic trying to find something *to* worry about.

More than 200 analgesic tablets to relieve headaches are on the market. Their basic ingredient is aspirin, but they may also contain caffeine, antacids, extra pain killers, antihistamines, vitamins, and tranquilizers. Yet scientists, following their comprehensive studies of headaches since World War II, have shown that most headaches represent the total personality in relation to the environment, and that it is often possible to adjust one's personality to end the headaches. According to headache experts, perhaps as many as ninety percent of headaches are precipitated by emotional factors. Tension headaches, they add, represent reaction to stress, usually an emotional stress. Sometimes it is physical, resulting from bad posture.

Anxious, hard-driving men and women, many doctors have suspected for some time, are more prone to heart attacks than their easygoing counterparts. Universtiy of Oklahoma researchers found that rats with brains electrically stimulated get cholesterol levels three to four times as high as those of normal rats, and high cholesterol levels have been related by many doctors to heart attacks.

Persons who later develop high blood pressure have one that rises easily with emotion and stays higher longer than average before returning to normal. But Dr. Dahl, of Brookhaven National Laboratory Research Centers Laboratory, labels "dubious" the idea that the stress and strain of daily living causes high blood pressure. Actually, it is *the wrong physiological language* which these people build up in themselves through chronic worry, anxiety, etc., from the effects of the stress and strain on their conscious minds, which brings on the tension headache. To relieve them, such people have to normalize their vehement physiological languages with the secret mental power to rout nagging pains and minor illness. This mental power can be triggered with the Miracle Mind Magic Stimulator.

How to Trigger Routing Your Nagging Aches
and Minor Illness with the Miracle Mind
Magic Stimulator

For decades doctors have successfully treated many patients successfully with brightly colored but inert capsules, called placebos. To add to their effect, these "wonder pills that do nothing" were usually made bitter or given an exotic name like "fluid extract of black cohosh." Doctors are amazed at the power of those blank pills to bring about not only improvement in the patient, but even to create some of the adverse side effects of actual drugs. Some patients will complain of trembling, dry mouth, vomiting, nausea, headache and drowsiness, and even skin rashes after taking such "empty pills." A group of diabetic patients on sulfa drugs was shown to maintain as good control with placebos.

Dr. Peart, one of the world's leading experts on high blood pressure, believes that, for some confusing reason, some drugs work with certain patients and not with others to reduce high blood pressure. It is obvious that the conscious mind—the secret mental power of the conscious mind—*is as potent as any drug*—for *none* of these patients was hypnotized! That same secret mental power can be triggered with the Miracle Mind Magic Stimulator. So, practice it and rout your own nagging aches and minor illness.

Sit alone in your room and visualize your own nagging aches and minor illness *vanishing completely* from your body, leaving you feeling sound and healthy again. That is your goal, dream, or wish. Hold that picture in mind for five seconds.

Then visualize that goal as coming true; visualize yourself changing completely and feeling as you did *before* you started suffering from these afflictions. Visualize yourself as the happy, pain-free person who looks at life with gusto and eagerness, and with a youthful enthusiasm to meet and overcome your every day challenges. Maintain that vision for four seconds.

Repeat that procedure three times, as you learned from practicing the Miracle Mind Magic Stimulator in Lesson 3. Intensify it each time, so you actually visualize yourself change *into that very same* pain-free, sickness-free person you were before. Rub each time, too, for a few seconds, right over the area of the minor ache, to *"rub it out of you"* while you visualize it vanishing in you. Practice until you need to visualize this former self of yours just once, for three seconds, for your physiological language to speak as it did when you were pain-free and well. Thereafter, you can trigger this secret mental power swiftly to rout nagging pains and minor illness.

Below are case histories of some who used this secret mental power to end their miseries. The names have been changed. Study them well and apply them even more effectively yourself.

How Edward A. Relieved His Nagging Headache
with a Simple Thought

Edward A. had suffered for years from a "heavy forehead" headache. He had resorted to pills, and had changed his collars, his hats, and even his jobs, but the misery persisted. He tried osteopaths, chiropractors, and naprapaths, too. Everything helped him at first—but only for a while. He grew so enraged at times that he felt like banging his head against a wall to "batter out" the torture.

I thought that his eyes might be to blame and urged him to consult with a specialist. He replied that his vision had been diagnosed as normal with the slightly corrected glasses he wore. So I told him that his posture was probably to blame. He carried his head too far forward and downward, and that dammed up the blood in his head and raised the blood pressure in it. He admitted that his orthopedist, his osteopath, and his chiropractor had pointed that out to him, but that it was difficult to remember always to keep his head normally high as he sat or walked.

I taught him that, whenever he had a headache, to hold one hand under his chin, with the nail of his index finger digging into the soft tissue like a spike. The sharp edge of his nail would straighten his head quickly.

To his astonishment Edward found that, whenever he did that, his headache soon went away, because he had straightened his head. But he couldn't do it in front of other people, he explained, particularly when standing or walking. So I had him imagine himself suffering from a head-splitting headache, and visualizing a spike (his nail) digging into his chin from below and "causing" the headache; and that, to get rid of the headache, he had to raise his head off that "spike."

Edward practiced doing that and came to associate his headache with the sharp "spike" below his chin. To reenforce that thought he used the Miracle Mind Magic Stimulator a few times a day to visualize himself as the happy, pain-free person who looked at life with gusto, eagerness, and youthful enthusiasm. Edward was soon controlling his maddening headache with a simple thought.

How Lena Y. Relieved Her Nagging Backache with a Simple Thought

Lena Y. had suffered for years from a nagging backache. Whether she remained at home as a housewife, worked, or went out socially or outdoors with her husband and family, it spoiled her fun and her efficiency. Not only that, but she had gone from one therapist to another, and all had found her back normal. But she insisted that she suffered terribly from it. Although her posture was passable, her shoulders pulled down hard and compressed her vertebrae and the spinal nerves which passed between them. One of her doctors had called her attention to that, she confessed, and had instructed her to stand erect. But how could she, she replied, when in action, which she was most of the time?

I taught Lena to visualize her spine, every time her back ached, as if it were a stiff rubber staff. That automatically forced her to stand straight. And when she went into action, it compelled her to hold her back as straight as she could. That prevented her shoulders from compressing her spine and her spinal nerves unduly. It also strengthened the muscles of her back, and particularly those of the spine (or the minute, but very important, although not popularized, myotomic muscles).

She practiced this and soon was doing it regularly. She also used the Miracle Mind Magic Stimulator to bring her upset physiological language back to normal. Her whole body felt so much better when she straightened it and kept it straightened, with its natural functions normalized, that she enjoyed tremendously the "stiff rubber staff" feeling of her spine and made it a permanent part of her. Her waist looked smaller, too, she looked taller, and her whole body younger and more graceful. Lena again found great pleasure with her family.

How Ray H. Relieved His "Bad" Stomach with a Simple Thought

Ray H. suffered from a "bad" stomach for years. Tests showed it to be normal, though, without ulcers or even gastritis. Psychiatry, too, diagnosed Ray as being even-tempered enough.

Yet, whenever he least expected it, he was belching and experiencing the flashy headaches attributed to stomach trouble.

I felt that Ray had a super-sensitive stomach; that is, one which turned acid easily after he ate and moved about, particularly after he consumed heavier foods with a high fat content, or stooped or bent down too soon after leaving the table. This acid tendency had been increased by daily tension, and his physiological language had altered into a fear-sympathetic control over his stomach which slowed down his digestion.

I taught Ray the secret mental power to rout nagging aches and minor illness, and he triggered the right physiological language for it with the Miracle Mind Magic Stimulator. His para-sympathetics then dominated him more and speeded up his digestion. He helped it along by diluting the acidity of his stomach all day long by imbibing about ten glasses of water. He also ate less heavy, fat-free foods. Ray's discomfort improved steadily and he felt like a different man thereafter when he triggered the simple thought with the Miracle Mind Magic Stimulator.

SUMMARY OF THIS SECRET MENTAL POWER

To rout your nagging aches and minor illness is to change yourself from an insufferable, defeated, frustrated, half-crazed person into a joyous, all-conquering, overwhelming, vibrantly alive one. To bring about such a change most easily in you, follow these simple routines:

1. If your nagging ache or minor illness is due to your daily unsuspected bad posture, correct it swiftly with the simple sharp spike thought.
2. If it is due to daily tensions, nullify their effects on you by triggering this secret mental power with the Miracle Mind Magic Stimulator.
3. These two exigencies will alter the physiological language of desperation with which your afflictions plague you, and change your whole mind and body to feel as you did when you were still pain-free and healthy.

Lesson 16

Secret Mental Power
for Sexual Vitality

If you are married, no matter how successfully you are achieving your goals, dreams, or wishes, or how free you are of nagging aches or minor illnesses, you live in an inferno on earth if you lack sexual vitality and marital bliss. (By sexual vitality is not meant abnormal sexual desire or activity, but the energy to satisfy your mate romantically.) Without these blessings your home is no heaven, and you dread the very thought of going back to it after work. You feel as though you are returning to a cruel jail after a brief parole. Your success in anything is dampened by the constant reminder that you cannot inspire the person you hold most dear, and your ego is crushed. Physiological demands are made on you at home which you fail to fulfill, and are followed by cat-and-dog fights. Yet you want a home and a loving companion, and someone with whom to enjoy your planned retirement. You are torn apart with frustration, and your desperate fight-sympathetics alter your physiological language into a venomous, panicky one.

You can alter this devastating situation swiftly with the secret mental power of sexual vitality and marital bliss. So, it is to your benefit to *master and apply it at once.*

The Amazing Gains from Sexual
Vitality and Marital Bliss

The gains of different people in their daily lives and in their careers from sexual vitality and marital bliss are miraculous. Many acquired bold personalities that converted them from low-paid shipping-room clerks into top company salesmen, drawing close to $200,000 a year. Others, from ignored social personalities, became the rage at parties. Many were super-charged with a new lease on life that rejuvenated them sensationally. A good number regained their zest for living, turned into dynamos during the day, and slept "like logs" at night. Still others acquired, in their games and hobbies, a steadiness of hand and eye that astounded their competitors and flooded themselves with new friends and admirers. Many who had lost their wit and social grace regained them and thrilled everybody they met. Others digested their food better, and their bowels moved better. Many stopped being tiresomely complaintive and started enjoying life. The list is limitless of how people changed themselves and their lives completely with the secret mental power for sexual vitality and marital bliss.

Why Your Domestic Familiarity Can Breed
Marital Contempt

Total domestic familiarity easily breeds marital contempt. It throws you and your mate so continuously together that you can no longer stimulate each other romantically. The sympathetic nervous system is the one to be aroused for sexual vitality, but too much familiarity suppresses it and leaves you calm, relaxed, and bovinely contented. Uncivilized people are noted for their low sexual vitality because their men and women habitually behold each other practically nude. Civilized people cover their bodies in public or expose only selected portions of them. That over-stimulates their sexual vitality and perhaps makes sex too great an issue in their everyday lives. But the comparison proves that overfamiliarity quenches the fires of desire. Total domestic familiarity does likewise for you because it alters your physiological language away from that of a sensual person. You become too "kind-hearted," too "self-sacrificial," and too paternal to be "devilishly" exciting. You lose the cavemannish drive to "take" what you want to enjoy, even if you momentarily have to act "brutal" to get it. You lose the capacity to turn into a cruel enough person (if you are a man), or into a hostile enough one (if you are a woman), to arouse the defiant sympathetics of your mate and bring on a delightful physical confrontation which leads to the ecstasy of furious conquest and rebellious submission.

Why Decreased Sexual Vitality Can Endanger Your Marital Bliss

When your sexual vitality is decreased by domestic familiarity, it breeds marital contempt—and marital contempt endangers your romantic bliss. Your decreased sexual vitality leads to romantic shyness of both of you, and your marriage degenerates into a brother-sister relationship, with correspondingly altered physiological languages dominated by your placid parasympathetics. Any time you want to be romantic you have to alter it completely. But that is not easy to do, for you have grown romantically shy. That's why so many people resort to heavy drinking bouts before they can "feel sexy." "Swingers," "swappers," so-called "healthy adultery," group sex, and similar relationships among increasing numbers of middle-aged people constitute extreme attempts of many to break down the tragically resulting sibling relationship of their harmonious marriages and to instill "viciousness" back into their love-making.

The fact that so many couples, according to psychologists, insist that such participations brought "spice" into their turned-sterile marriages, and even saved many from "the rocks," proves that even the young and sexually vigorous suffer from reduced sexual vitality due to total domestic familiarity. Sexual vitality, in other words, can be reduced by the *conscious mind!* It can therefore also be regained by the conscious mind!

Why You Have to Add Ecstasy to Your Domestic Familiarity

To add ecstasy to your domestic familiarity you have to change your acquired unreactive physiological language toward

202 Secret Mental Power for Sexual Vitality

your mate. You have to surcharge your whole body—*all* your organs, not just your sex organs—with the youthful eagerness that can fill your mate with bliss. Love, after all, is an emotional reaction. You cannot love your husband or wife *scientifically.*

How true is the old saying that "love is blind." It has to be blind enough to overlook all the picayune imperfections of your mate, for nobody is perfect. You can't look at your loved one with a microscope when you want to add ecstasy to your romantic relationship. You have to look with the eyes of the enthralled poet or worshipper (or enchanter) who refashions everything about his adored into the acme of perfection. Such an attitude is the farthest thing from that of a scientist. But it is the most potent stimulator of sexual vitality in you, and the surest one to make a paradise of your home.

And this is why. When you regard your adored one with such eyes, your conscious mind alters your physiological language into that of such a person! Rapturous phrases gush from you then which you could not create if you sat down coolly and tried to. Your manner, your attitude, your wit, your sensitivity; indeed, your every action and demeanor, change into that of a totally different person. No longer are you still just the romantically-boring, brotherly-like provider (if you are a man), but the dashing, appetizing, conquering Don Juan himself! (If you are a woman, you are changed into a bewitching Cleopatra!) Your heart beats faster, your lungs breathe faster, your mouth waters, your nerves flash dynamically into your tissues, and your brain and body come vibrantly alive with the aggression of the irresistible lover. New, oxygen-rich blood pours rejuvenating hormones into your brain, which are let loose by your new, gland-stimulating physiological language. These incite the neurons of your conscious mind with daring and exciting ideas. These, in turn, flash commands to your muscles, and you move forward to conquer. You are no longer the fraternal mate, but the love-magnet, the love-machine. That's why you *have* to add ecstasy to your domestic familiarity.

How Your Usual Mental Attitude Bars
Ecstasy from Your Domestic Familiarity

Your usual mental attitude bars ecstasy from your domestic familiarity for many reasons. It represses it with the mores of the society you live in, with the laws you are aware of, with your past frustrations, romantically, socially or in business; with your supersensitive recollections of rebuffs, real or imagined, which you have suffered in the past and which you fear might occur again; with your previous failures or dissatisfactions in your relationship with your mate; with your lack of absolute confidence in your own sexual vigor; with your secret anxiety over your "waning appeal," resulting mainly from your overawareness of "growing older," of graying, wrinkling, or even balding; with the infuriating realization that you might never develop into the big money maker you had hoped to become and, therefore, can't expect to do all you had secretly hoped to do for your loved ones.

These and similar philosophical adjustments to life build up a psychological barrier around your spontaneous behavior that is as difficult to break through as an encasing pipe. They keep your romantic behavior enslaved in a strait jacket and feed upon themselves. Whenever you try to break free from them and find that you can't, your heart beats like mad and you lose your breath. Dread of failure overtakes you, and you might even break out in the cold sweat of terror. Even your throat and tongue cramp, and you can hardly utter a sound. Your physiological language has altered into that of a romantic impotent. That's why your usual mental attitude bars ecstasy from your domestic familiarity.

How to Overcome the Influence of Your Usual Mental Attitude Which Bars Ecstasy from Your Domestic Familiarity

To overcome the handicaps of your usual mental attitude and add ecstasy to your domestic familiarity, you have to change the fear-stricken physiological language it creates in you into an advance-and-conquer one. To do so, stop thinking about romance and visualize every muscle in your body, from head to foot, turning into putty. "Feel" the very hair on your scalp lie back down, the tenseness of your brow ease, the fixity in your eyes soften, your hardbiting jaw hang loose, your tense tongue and neck relax, your shoulders droop easily, your torso become bland, your crouching back smooth out, your arms dangle easily, your hands unclench fully, your legs become flexible, and your toes stop gripping the ground. Practice this to grow keenly aware of your relaxing every one of these tension-triggering muscles, so they will discharge into your brain, instead, all the nerve-electricity they have locked up in them. Practice it until you can relax them all in three seconds, then two, and finally in one second.

Your heart will slow down swiftly then, and your breathlessness will leave you. Your brain will flush with blood, and the waste products resulting from your terror and frustration will be washed out of it and new, young, oxygen-filled, properly hormoned blood will replace it. In no time, you will overcome the influence of your usual mental attitude which bars ecstasy from your domestic familiarity.

How to Add Ecstasy to Your Domestic Familiarity

To add ecstasy to your domestic familiarity, change your physiological language into that of an advance-and-conquer lover. To accomplish that, command your sympathetics from a parasympathetics frame of mind. Command them, in other words, not to conquer like a soldier killing on the battlefield, but like a gourmet devouring a delicious meal. Fill your eyes with the eagerness of the predator; your lips with the taste of the glutton; your arms with the feel of the conqueror (or bewitcher, if you are a woman); and the rest of your body with the readiness to overthrow (or spellbind, if you are a woman). Stare at your mate no longer with the brotherly (or sisterly) manner of before, but like a pleasure-seeking *stranger.* The feeling of strangeness *must be felt* in order to change your physiological language toward your mate.

This feeling of yours stuns your mate and also her (or his) physiological language away from the placid, too-brotherly parasympathetics one. And so, you two feel like strangers confined to your private quarters now, itching to combat each other for corporeal superiority. You have added ecstasy to your romantic familiarity. You will be charged with sexual vitality and be ready to enjoy explosive marital bliss.

How to Trigger Sexual Vitality and Marital Bliss with the Miracle Mind Magic Stimulator

To trigger yourself into this secret mental power most swiftly, apply the Miracle Mind Magic Stimulator before you even commence it. Sit alone in your room and visualize your regular self changing from a nonentity romantically to a most sensationally satisfying husband (or wife). That is your goal, dream, or wish. Hold that picture in your mind for five seconds.

Then visualize that goal as coming true; visualize yourself changing completely and feeling as you *would* feel if you were suddenly changed into that kind of person. Visualize yourself facing your mate, bursting with eagerness to conquer (her) or ensnare (him). Maintain that vision for four seconds.

Repeat that procedure three times, as you learned from practicing the Miracle Mind Magic Stimulator in Lesson 3. Intensify it each time, so you actually visualize and *feel* yourself change into such a person. Practice getting this sensation of changing into him until your eyes fill with the eagerness of the delighted predator, your mouth and lips with the taste of the revelling glutton, your hands with the feel of the overjoyed conqueror (or bewitcher), and the rest of you with the readiness to overthrow (or spellbind). Practice until you need to visualize it but once, in three seconds, for your physiological language to speak like that of such a person. You can then trigger the secret mental power for sexual vitality and marital bliss swiftly thereafter and *be* the conqueror or enslaver.

Below are case histories of some who used this secret mental power for everyday gain. Their names have been changed. Study them and gain even more from them.

How Phillip R. Changed from a Low-Paid Shipping-Room Clerk to a Top Company Salesman Earning Over $100,000 a Year

Phillip R. was sick and tired of being a low-paid shipping-room clerk. "I was surely born for something better than this!" he moaned. As a young man he had dropped out of college and was faring like so many others with similar fates. He had dreamed of "the luxurious life," but without a college degree, trade, or profitable occupation, he had been forced to seek odd or unskilled work. Finally, he had settled for a shipping-room clerk's position. Had he aspired for nothing more, he could have been satisfied; but to watch his former college classmates rise high in big posts or in the leading professions, while he himself remained a nobody. His anger over his past mistakes mounted. He *should* have stayed in college over thirty years ago, he raged, no matter how boring and loaded with homework it had been. He could hardly endure going to work anymore.

His bitter dissatisfaction had repercussions at home. His sexual vitality vanished, and his wife resented his general attitude toward life. "You talk as if you're too good for your work!" she cried. "Somebody has to dig the ditches, too! Hard work never hurt anybody! Everybody isn't college material! Big money isn't the only thing to live for, anyhow! Honest work is still honest work!"

I realized that Phillip was not consoled by such reasoning. I myself did not consider him the student type. Yet he was sensitive and ambitious.

I taught him the secret mental power for sexual vitality and marital bliss. With it Phillip subdued his dissatisfied mental attitude, and triggered his sexual vitality with the Miracle Mind Magic Stimulator. That altered his fear-filled physiological language into that of a romantic conqueror. His wife was thrilled.

Next day Phillip was bursting with enthusiasm and confidence in his "great" abilities and applied to his company as a salesman. His new, conquering manner brought him swift success and turned his home into a paradise. In less than three years he was earning $100,000 a year.

How Alvin Z., Who Had Trouble Sleeping,
Slept at Night Like a Log

Alvin Z. suffered from insomnia (sleeplessness) for a long time. His psychiatrist found his mental attitude normal, and his marital relationship satisfactory. But he was surprised that Alvin had relations with his wife so infrequently and encouraged him to do so more often, to induce normal sleep without pills.

Phillip tried to obey him, but could hardly arouse himself with Ina. Ashamed to return to his psychiatrist, he confessed to me that, although he was happy and contented with his wife, the prospect of sex with her plagued him with a fear-stricken physiological language that robbed him of aggression.

To overcome it, I taught him the secret mental power for sexual vitality and marital bliss. He practiced it thoroughly and filled his eyes with the eagerness of the predator, his lips with the taste of the glutton, his arms with the feel of the conqueror, and the rest of his body with the readiness to overthrow. He stared at Ina no longer in the brotherly manner of yore, but like a pleasure-seeking *stranger.* He practiced all this so well that he *felt* that feeling of strangeness, and it changed his physiological language toward Ina.

Alvin's change from the placid, too-brotherly attitude stunned Ina, and they felt like strangers confined to Alvin's private quarters, itching to combat each other for physical superiority. Charged now with sexual vitality, Alvin sallied after Ina like a conqueror.

He slept like a log afterward. Thereafter he required no more drugs to fall asleep.

How Harold A. Became a Hungrily-Wanted
Husband with a Master Mental Move

Harold A. had done remarkably well in his career, and his wife, Helen, was free of family responsibilities now that their youngest daughter was married. For the first time since their newlywed days, they had each other for themselves. And yet Harold had the peculiar feeling that the woman in his bed was no intimate part of his life. Helen was still very attractive, though. When Harold married her he had expected their love to endure all their lives. Instead, they had drifted apart and no longer showed affection or intimacy with each other. They quarreled often, in fact, and blamed each other on their inability to communicate with each other.

With the children and older parents no longer around the house, they engaged in prolonged arguments, followed by bitter silences. Matters had deteriorated to such a degree that Harold secretly considered carrying on an affair.

He made a desperate effort to save their home, but failed. He lacked sexual vigor, he confessed to me, and Helen was badly upset by it.

I taught Harold the secret mental power for sexual vitality and marital bliss. He mastered it fast and, with the Miracle Mind Magic Stimulator, altered his vacillating physiological language into an advance-and-conquer one, ruled by his aggressive sympathetics. His sexual vitality zoomed, for he now saw Helen as a strange, entrancing female, imprisoned by him in their quarters. His attitude changed from that of an embarrassed, hesitant, self-conscious brotherly old husband into that of a demanding young pursuer. Helen's own frustrated physiological language altered as a result, and she responded in kind. They embarked upon a second honeymoon. It was even more exciting than their first, for now they felt a new sense of freedom and abandon in lovemaking, as there was no need to fear conception or interruption by small children in the home.

SUMMARY OF THIS SECRET MENTAL POWER

To regain your sexual vitality and enjoy marital bliss is to change your whole life from a frightened, unpleasant one into a life of thrills and excitement, without even leaving your home. To bring about this change in you most easily, follow these simple routines:

1. To regain your sexual vitality and attain marital bliss, overcome your usual mental attitude which bars ecstasy from your domestic familiarity.
2. Then add ecstasy to your domestic familiarity.
3. Then trigger your sexual vitality and its resulting marital bliss with the Miracle Mind Magic Stimulator.
4. Your placid or fearful physiological language will be altered into that of a romantic conquerer (or ensnarer).

How to Use Secret Mental Powers to Stay Younger and Live Longer

When you are pursuing or have achieved your goals, dreams, or wishes, to enjoy your gains sufficiently you have to stay young and live long. To stay young and live long, your body has to speak the physiological language of youth. Your organs then feel young because they function as though you *are* young. After all, they can live in a test tube for a much longer time than your life span. Even when you die your organs are not dead. They die later, because your blood has stopped circulating and no longer brings them oxygen and nutrition or removes their waste products. When you die, then, your body is not an old, dying body.

Your arteries may harden and form a blood clot that stops your heartbeat, but your hair, your skin, your eyes, your teeth, your heart itself, your kidneys, your glands, your stomach—in fact, *every remaining part* of you is still as much alive as before you expired. They are *still* comparatively young, in other words. And these other parts represent about ninety-eight percent of you. You are then, to be exact, a young person whose body no longer functions like someone alive. That's why you *can* stay young and live long. And your mind can do it for you because physiologists have found that *it can even dissolve blood clots.* So, master this secret mental power!

The Fantastic Profits from Staying Young and Living Long

To stay young and live long are fantastic profits in themselves. But they can also bring equally fantastic profits, in addition. People who made serious mistakes in life and got nowhere until their middle age used their past experiences when they were as old as fifty-six or sixty-four and became multi-millionaires—or even billionaires. (The well-known case of C. S. Penney is but one example.) Others attained the most exalted positions in their careers. Actress Mae West was finished in her thirties, but came back near age eighty as a sensational "sex bomb." George Bernard Shaw and Alexandre Dumas were practically unpublished unknowns until their middle forties, and then attained fame and fortune as literary men. Desperate inventors who got nowhere until their fifties "hit the jackpot." Heavyweight "Jersey" Joe Walcott fought in the ring for fifteen years and gained little, but at thirty-seven he was champion and lost the title only to the much-younger, never-to-be-defeated Rocky Marciano. By staying alive until his eighties, a man was elected premier of France and was a great one. Many average men, by living long, enjoyed retirement on their pensions for thirty or forty years. Others returned to college in their fifties, were professional men in their sixties, and lived thereafter in affluence and respect *and practiced only when they wished to!*

Others formed sects that spread around the world. None of these people would have achieved much in life had they not stayed young enough and lived long enough. So, study this secret mental power carefully! You won't enjoy the rewards of your efforts in anything unless you keep yourself young enough, physiologically, to live long.

The Physiological Language That Keeps You Young

To keep young, your mind and body have to speak a flexible physiological language. You can't let your body speak a "fixed" physiological language which does not adjust efficiently to each experience you have. You have to "speak" a powerful fight-

sympathetic physiological language, for instance, when you are sick or face immediate danger. But you can't speak that same physiological language in your everyday life and expect to stay young and live long, because it will exhaust you with nervous tension, deplete your muscles with "overtone strain," weary your heart with overbeating, ruin your stomach with indigestion, and torture your brain with worry. (In women, in fact, there is commonly found a high blood pressure due to sympathetics' stimulation. It is therefore believed that prolonged sympathetics dominance could result in hardening of the arteries.)

You will fare no better if your mind and body speak a fixed, powerful, *love-para*sympathetic physiological language which keeps you so "idiotically resigned" to everything that your body won't even fight off disease, or your mind won't solve difficult problems or try to achieve anything, but just leaves you tinkering with one idle interest after another.

Your mind and body have to speak a flexible physiological language that will adjust you to your experiences and keep you young; one that never lets you grow old and staid, unable to adjust to new changes and trends, and to different people and novel life situations.

How Your Two Involuntary Nervous Systems
May Fail to Keep You Speaking the
Physiological Language of Youth

Your sympathetic and parasympathetic nervous systems automatically attempt to keep your mind and body speaking the physiological language of youth by continually trying to prevent each other from dominating you. Whenever your heart beats too fast (or when overstimulated by your sympathetics), your parasympathetics slow it down. Whenever it beats too slowly (such as when you are drugged or gassed, or feeling sick or tired), your sympathetics speed it up. Whenever your muscles are overtensed from fright, from worry, or from nervousness (being overstimulated by your sympathetics), your parasympathetics sap the excess tension out of them. Whenever anything at all abnormalizes your physiological language (and leaves one of your involuntary nervous systems overstimulating you), your other involuntary nervous system brings it back to normal. They save you from going to extremes and, thereby, stave off exhaustion and old age.

As you grow older, though, and acquire different leanings, prejudices, likes and dislikes, fears, and blind adorations, one of your two involuntary nervous systems predominates in you on occasion and carries over into other occasions until it *slants your whole physiology and personality* in its direction. There *are* sympatheticotonic and parasympatheticotonic patients. The sympatheticotonic is clinically diagnosed for his refusal to rest or "slow down." By the time he reaches the doctor's office he is suffering from exhaustion of his sympathetic nervous system and his adrenal glands. He shows this with his indigestion, low blood pressure (because his heart is beating so fast that his blood pressure falls), asthenia (weakness and debility), nervous break-down, neurasthenia (nervous exhaustion), or collapse. He is treated with rest, with a new mental outlook (to balance his physiological language), with plain but attractive food well masticated, with avoidance of all excitement and worry, and with the abstinence of sexual relations (since these overstimulate his sympathetics). He is difficult to treat, however, because his mind and imagination are so active and fired with ambition that he can't gain the maximum from physical rest.

His opposite is the parasympatheticotonic (or vagotonic) patient. He is so placid that he lacks ambition for anything that requires effort; enjoys eating all day long; hates exercise and, therefore, becomes overweight easily. Hence, he is prone to catarrh, asthma, stomach upsets, overeating and eating just what he thinks he likes, spastic constipation, diabetes, infections (because his sympathetics don't stimulate his physiological lan-guage strongly enough to combat disease), and obesity.

Although those are naturally born cases, you *can* degenerate into one yourself if your life experiences, your bad habits, your type of thinking, and other unbalancing factors cause a chronic predominance of one of these involuntary nervous systems in you and slant your physiology and personality in its direction.

The Three Magic Secrets to Stay Young and
Live Long with a Flexible Physiological
Language

Magic Secret 1: How to Control Your
Appetite and Keep Your Weight Normal
with a Simple Thought

When your appetite is outside your control, especially for
fattening foods, it means that your physiological language is not
flexible. You are parasympatheticotonic then, with an abnormal
taste for sweets, fried foods, desserts, fancy bakery concoctions,
and other unhealthy delights. Or you are sympatheticotonic and
gripped with nervous tension, frustration, dread, or impatience,
and overeat to compensate for it. Either way your physiological
language is not flexible, and excess food energy is deposited in
your body cells and turns to fat. To combat this peril you have to
control your appetite with a flexible physiological language.

This is how to do it. Instead of gobbling your food
voraciously (with parasympatheticotonia), or in a panicky way
(panic-eating with fear- or dread-sympathetics), concentrate
instead on some other intriguing problem. Take your mind off
your food and its taste, in other words, so you stop tasting it or
worrying about it. Chew long and slowly, too, and tire your jaws.
Your overeager (to swallow your food) conscious mind will stop
over-stimulating your salivary and gastric glands. Do likewise with
mouthful after mouthful and alter the controlling thought beat of
your digestive system. That will slow it down, just as your thought
beat slows down your heartbeat. Your appetite will lessen, and
your salivary and gastric glands will gradually shrink in size. Your
body, as a result, will assimilate less food, and you will lose
weight. Any time you start gaining weight thereafter, resume the
"though-beat eating habit," and keep your weight down permanently. You will be astonished at its miraculous effects.

Magic Secret 2: The Trick to Regain
Youthful Sex Appeal with a Simple Thought

Your conscious mind holds the prime control over your
regaining your physiological language of youth and longevity, for

you cannot regain that physiological language unless you think well of yourself. Tests by psychologists Keisler and Baral of Connecticut College proved that male subjects who thought well of themselves tended to choose prettier girls for dates than male subjects who thought less well of themselves. Forty-eight unmarried men were given individual I.Q. tests, on which they were told they were doing well or poorly, regardless of their actual performances.

Those who were told they did well on the fake tests pursued the more attractive girls during the coffee breaks, while those who were told they were doing poorly pursued the less attractive ones. Those who did "well" did not acquire their confidence in themselves because they thought they were more handsome or wealthy than before, but because they thought they were *more intelligent.* Yet, they were only *fooled* into thinking that they were. As the researchers put it, it gave them a high self-esteem.

What occurred in these young men when their self-esteem went up? Simply this. Their vacillating physiological languages altered into youthful-aggressive ones in which their hearts beat strongly but calmly, their breathing was full and natural, their muscles relaxed but surged with subtle energy, and the arteries of their brains widened to let fresh blood pour oxygen and nutrition into them and wash out their fears, doubts, tensions, and instabilities. The fooled young men, as a consequence, burst forth irresistibly!

How to Regain Your Own Youthful Sex Appeal with a Simple Thought

Sit alone in your room and visualize yourself again when young enough to be at your most appealing. Visualize, too, the person whom you adored most then romantically, but whom you had little chance with. (Youth has long since left that person, but still visualize him as he looked then.) Visualize yourself changing now into the person *whom you should have looked and been like then* to enthrall that unattainable romantic partner. (People and sex appeal don't change; what was romantically appealing then would be appealing now.) Proceed now in your visualization, and *conquer* that unattainable partner romantically *in any way* you feel it could have been done.

Now visualize yourself leaping out of that gone world. But remain *exactly as you have just changed yourself in it to conquer that unattainable partner.* Fool yourself, in brief, into feeling that you always *did* conquer all your unattainable romantic partners in the past, and let your physiological language alter into that of such a person.

Go out into the world, now, feeling and acting *like such a person.* You will find yourself staggeringly attractive, and acting as young as ever.

*Magic Secret 3: How to Stimulate Your Body
Cells to Defy Aging with a Simple Thought*

You can stay young and live long by fooling your physiological language into believing that you are much younger than you are, and that you will live much longer than expected to. To do so, fill your conscious mind with the conviction that you really *are* much younger than your birth certificate reads, in your body tissues if not in years. If you are wrinkling or graying, blot these facts out of your mind and think of yourself as being without wrinkles and with your hair still having its natural color. Practice doing this until you "convince" yourself that this is so, just as the fooled students taking the I.Q. tests were convinced that they *were* smarter than they really were. A great burden will fall off your shoulders, and your physiological language will change instantly from the repressed, uncertain, back-seat-taking one of accepting aging apologetically, into the bold, positive, conquering one of eternal youth. That will create an atmosphere about you which will "infect" the other person and alter his mind about you. *You* will note that by the different way he looks at you, and that will rejuvenate your whole physiological language still more. You will then burst forth with the confident beating heart and the physical virility of recaptured youth.

(That whole cycle reduces the "old age virulence" of your fight-sympathetics—which are heavily acid-producing—and thus dilutes the acid cathepsins which accumulate naturally in your body cells as you grow older and multiply after death. That defies natural aging! All with a simple thought! Orient yourself to thinking of still being young, or of being much younger than you are, and your conscious mind will direct your physiological language to speak the tongue of youth. Your every tissue will be affected by that change and will become younger whether they "wish to" or not.)

How to Trigger Your Staying Young and Living Long with the Miracle Mind Magic Stimulator

Trigger yourself into youth and longevity every morning when you arise, and repeatedly during the day. Trigger it every time you meet anybody or encounter anything that presents an obstacle to you and threatens you with failure. Trigger it with the Miracle Mind Magic Stimulator. It will alter your physiological language into that of the person you were when you were much younger.

Your Personal Program

To practice the Miracle Mind Magic Stimulator sit alone in your room and visualize yourself changing completely into the person you were twenty-five or thirty years ago, or whenever you were at your healthiest and most attractive *as an adult.* (Don't try to visualize yourself back in your teens, because your subconscious mind might reject that picture.) That is your goal, dream, or wish. Hold that picture in your mind for five seconds.

Then visualize that goal as coming true; visualize yourself changing completely and feeling as you *would* feel if suddenly changed like that. Maintain that vision for four seconds.

Repeat that procedure three times, as you learned from practicing the Miracle Mind Magic Stimulator in Lesson 3. Intensify it each time, so you actually visualize and *feel* your whole mind and body change into the *you* you were then. Visualize it so *realistically* that you feel your whole mind and body bursting with the energy, with the eagerness, with the confidence with people, with the muscle tone, with the healthy appetite, with the force of mind, with the sexual vitality, and even with the appearance, skin, and hair you possessed then! *Forget what you are or look like now. Become again as you were back then! Become it so absolutely that you no longer think or see yourself as you are now.* Practice *becoming* like that until you need to visualize it just once, in three seconds, for your physiological language to change and speak the language of youth (youth takes care of longevity). You will trigger easily thereafter this secret mental power and change yourself as completely from what you are now as those unmarried men changed themselves into sex conquerors with their new, fraudulently-induced, high self-esteem.

Below are case histories of some who used this secret mental power for everyday profit. Study them well, and gain even more than they in your own day-to-day living.

How Middle-Aged Jane L. Stayed Young Despite Her Youth-Robbing Work

After Jane L., like so many women, read Frank Young's *Yoga for Men Only*, she concluded that, to stay young and live long, one had to protect himself continually against the unintentional attempts of others to abuse him at work and rob him of youth and longevity. Since your boss wields abnormal power over you, you have to protect yourself against him. Every day at work, Jane's boss made demands upon her that prevented her from caring for herself as she would like to. Too frequently she had to work faster than she wished, could not drink enough water to keep her stools soft, had to sit or stand too long at a time (both of which wearied her and contributed to constipation, hemorrhoids, and varicose veins), and to strain her eyes against lights that were either too glaring or not bright enough. These inescapable aggravations and many more put Jane's normal physiological language chronically under predominance of her fear- and anger-sympathetics; fear of invoking her boss' displeasure if she complained against them, and anger of fearing his retaliatory powers if she complained.

Since she could do little to alter the situation, for she realized that her boss had to watch rising production costs, Jane approached me in despair. I agreed with her that her working conditions should be improved. I also explained, however, that many slaves and serfs had labored like beasts, and yet managed to stay young and live even beyond 120. They were called "good-natured" by those who knew them; but actually they had learned, philosophically or otherwise, what amounted to maintaining a perfect balance between their sympathetics and their parasympathetics, and thereby how to keep their physiological languages normal all their lives.

That secret predisposed them against developing primary high blood pressure (which is due to spasm of the circular muscles of the little arteries). That, in its turn, saved their hearts from being overburdened with strenuous blood pumping, their kidneys from excess filtering, and their brains from receiving less oxygen than they needed (because high blood pressure reduces the amount of blood flowing into the head). Their whole bodies, as a result, stayed much younger than those of similar victims who raged at their plight and thereby unbalanced their physiological languages.

So I taught Jane the secret mental power to stay young and live long. She learned it fast and triggered it daily, at work, with the Miracle Mind Magic Stimulator. It kept her physiological language *normal*, even when she had to hurry "like mad" during the rush hour or the rush season. That leveled her blood pressure and calmed her digestion. She started feeling better *at once*—and looking younger. Ten years later Jane looks *younger* than she did nearly twenty years ago, when she was first employed by the company.

*How Fifty-Nine-Year-Old Peter D. Regained
His Lost Energy and "Youth" Speedily and
Re-entered the Dynamic Life Stream*

At fifty-nine, Peter D. was a mass of nagging aches and pains. His energy had gone, and he felt as if death was long overdue. He lived on tonics and stimulants, envied bitterly every young person he saw, and was outraged that any of them had "the gall" to complain about anything whatsoever when they could walk, run, eat their fill, enjoy sex, and perform the other natural functions of the body without giving them a second thought. But *he himself*, he raved, could hardly walk a step without aching in the knees and back, and much less run. With food, the least thing set his stomach burping. For sex? "Don't make me laugh!" he snorted. Even to sleep or relax he needed tranquilizers. To make his bowels move he was enslaved to laxatives, enemas, and other "insufferable things." And yet, he fumed, his doctor said he was not really sick!

I taught Peter the secret mental power to stay young and live long. His physiological language was most unhealthily ruled, I told him, by his physical torments. These had resulted from the usual unavoidable internal "bruises" caused by the "blows" dealt him regularly by the bad average posture he had acquired from his daily inefficient body mechanics. "Blows," also, by his slowing down metabolism and other inescapable alterations in his body physiology resulting from his lifetime of typical health abuse. All together, they had overstimulated his anger-sympathetics in his rage against the torments, and his fear-sympathetics in his dread of the possible future ills they foreboded.

I taught Peter the secret mental power to stay young and live long. He learned it fast and triggered it with the Miracle Mind Magic Stimulator. In very short order it normalized his fulminating physiological language. That pacified his nerves and reduced the intensity of his physical torments. His heartbeat, his blood pressure, and his hypertensed muscles relaxed. With his sympathetics and parasympathetics balanced again, his sex organs were once more supplied normally with blood and his natural inclinations returned. Peter felt and thought, now, like a much younger man. His food digested better, carried more nutriments to his whole body, and restored his lost energy. He saw a woman who fascinated him, re-entered the dynamic lifestream and won her, three months later, as his wife.

SUMMARY OF THIS SECRET MENTAL POWER

To stay young and live long is actually to *"reincarnate"* yourself into a *second life* and start enjoying what you missed out on before. To bring about this enchanting change most easily in you, follow these simple routines:

1. Set out to help your two involuntary nervous systems (your sympathetics and your parasympathetics) balance themselves and make your mind and body speak the physiological language of youth.
2. Do so by ending the inferiority-creating dominance of

your aging fear- and dread-sympathetics over you and become again the person you were when young.

3. Trigger this change in you with the Miracle Mind Magic Stimulator.

4. It will change your physiological language from one of "getting old" to one of staying young and living long.

Instant Physio-Magic: The Secret of Perpetual Miracle Mind Magic

Although each secret mental power brings you a different miracle of mind magic, you can trigger *any* of them with Instant Physio-Magic. You can then apply *any* of them at any time to make any goal, dream, or wish come true. You will possess a conscious mind as dominating as the most irresistible hypnotist, the most fantastic psychic, the most prophetic seer, the strongest Hercules—or of a genius in anything you strive for! With it, as others did, you can change an average mind into that of a genius *instantly*! You can acquire the power of a lion (like a hypnotized subject) instantly! You can acquire enthralling romantic appeal instantly! You can do all that because, with Instant Physio-Magic, you can swiftly speak the *right physiological language* for *any* secret mental power you wish. *You then become the person who possesses that secret mental power.* So, master Instant Physio-Magic.

The Three Secret Steps of Instant Physio-Magic

Step 1: Visualize clearly and *fearlessly* the goal, dream, or wish you want to come true.

Step 2: Visualize it coming true instantly, with every

obstacle in your path being easily crushed (even if you have to "stretch" your imagination to do so).

Step 3: Visualize yourself, now, as becoming *the* person who *can* realize this goal, dream, or wish *without any effort whatever!* (If you know such a person yourself, visualize yourself *becoming him!*) Visualize your physiological language changing to be *like his*, so you think, act, speak, and move *just like him.*

Practice and *master* these three steps.

The Magic Power of the Three Secret Steps to Get What You Want, for Nothing

Behind the three secret steps of Instant Physio-Magic lies the miracle of mind magic of every secret mental power. It is the secret of *getting for yourself what you want for nothing.* With Instant Physio-Magic, to put it simply, you visualize your goal, dream, or wish as coming true *even before* your physiological language speaks the right tongue you need to achieve it. *You then get something for nothing* because you get it *before* you are qualified for it!

That's exactly how those average students became "geniuses" when their fooled teacher *taught them* as though they *were* geniuses. That's exactly how the nonhypnotized equalled the power feats of the hypnotized subjects. That's exactly how the unmarried men *without* high I.Q.'s pursued and dated the most attractive girls after being misled into believing that their I.Q.'s were high. In each instance, the individuals had been deceived into believing they had powers which they didn't have! So they *got* something for nothing! And they got it *instantly.*

The Miracle of Instant Physio-Magic

With the miracle of Instant Physio-Magic no goal, dream, or wish of yours, no matter how fantastic, will seem outside your reach. That in itself snatches you out of the average class into the master class which compares with the mystic and his magic rod, the hypnotist and his commanding word, the psychic master and his miracle-creating simple thought. All these, too, *get something for nothing*. They may get it through a magic power, but your conscious mind is also a magic power. You regularly use only a small fraction of it, for one thing, and it is far more capable than the most advanced computer. Yet it is only a mass of nerve tissue. But when you release it with the full force of your Secret Mental Powers, *you turn into a man (or woman) of miracles overnight!*

Step-by-Step Method for Using the New Miracle-Mind You

Here, step-by-step, is how to use the new miracle-mind you in everyday life and achieve your every goal, dream, or wish *for nothing*.

1. Whenever you are weighted down with unhappy moods, convert yourself instantly, with intellectual leverage, into a calm, contented person.
2. If you aren't making the money you want in your career because of something you "lack," overcome and prevent confused thinking and hit the big time fast.
3. To figure out new avenues to stupendous profits, make miracle use of the sixteen secret rules for profitable concentration.
4. When torn to shreds with worry, banish it with the thought beat.
5. When anybody tries to dominate you, tear yourself free with the secret Clench and Relax.
6. Whenever you want to dominate someone swiftly, make his mind and body speak *your* physiological language.
7. When about to lose your temper and imperil your every gain, control it with the most sensible judgment.
8. To grow rich "like lightning," apply perfect timing.
9. To overcome a nagging ache, think one simple thought.
10. To feel wanted at home for *yourself,* add ecstasy to your domestic familiarity.
11. To escape economic disaster, swiftly learn a new, wanted skill expertly.
12. If jobs or people ignore you because you are "getting old," become again the person you were when young.

13. If a bully accosts you, "disarm" him with intellectual leverage.
14. If you are helpless before the mate you want, master the situation with new sexual vitality.

IN CONCLUSION

Select *the* secret mental power which you desire most right now and reread and repractice it. Select two or three if you can't decide on one. (Reread any of the others whenever you need them.) When you practice any of them, be keenly aware of how it alters your physiological language. You don't have to listen to your heartbeat each time, but always *feel* like a person who *could easily* achieve your goal, dream, or wish. Always imagine yourself as *becoming* him (or her) and then note *exactly how you feel! Imitate everything* about him when you do, so you no longer feel like yourself, *but wholly like him*! That's when you will *think* like him, when your physiological language will *speak* like his, and when the particular secret mental power which *he* would use to achieve a goal, dream, or wish like yours *will become yours, too*! You will then possess the miracle of mind magic.

Physiological language. This means the way your mind and body react normally or abnormally to anything. If you are happy, it reacts one way. If you are sad, it reacts the opposite way. If you are defiant, it reacts one way. If you are terrified, it reacts the opposite way. Your mind and body, therefore, may be said to speak a physiological language which adapts itself to your different experiences.

Sympathetic nervous system. This is the nervous system in you that speeds up your heart, etc., when your physiological language is stimulated to send you into fight, or to take to flight, including all emotions related to them, such as anger, fear, dread, terror, submission, etc.

Parasympathetic nervous system. This is the nervous system in you that slows down your heart, etc., when your physiological language is stimulated to be peaceful and contented, including all emotions related to them, such as cheer, humor, love, appetite, etc.

Get Published!

"Everyone has something they know well or can do well. And when a person has a skill, there's always going to be someone willing to pay for it."

parkerpub.co

Parker Publishing Company helps authors publish more titles. So whether you're writing a metaphysical, romance novel, a historical fiction, a mystery, action or suspense story, poetry, business, a children's book, or any other writer, we can help you reach your publishing goals.

Since 1960 we've offered a unique publishing experience to Authors, all over the world. Parker Publishing Company wants to help new authors in all aspects of publishing. The editing, marketing, multi-media design and copyright production and enforcement. From eBooks, Paperback, Hardcovers to Audiobooks can be produced in small volumes and offered to the public.

Besides telling a story, a book is a promotional tool. A book can be likened to a powerful business card since most people won't throw it out. Authoring a book can give you credibility and status, enabling you to charge more for your services.

Your writing will reach more than 20,000 retail accounts worldwide (chains, independents, specialty stores, and libraries). Our United States, Australia and United Kingdom-based sales teams work with clients all over the world through our broad distribution channel partners. For more information please contact us at **www.parkerpub.co**

PARKER
PUBLISHING COMPANY

PUBLISHING COMPANY